40 DAYS

*Inspiration and Encouragement
to Get You Through Tough Times*

THERESE MARSZALEK

40 Days:
Inspiration and Encouragement to Get You Through Tough Times

ISBN: 978-1-936314-37-9
Copyright © 2011 by Therese Marszalek
21616 No. Spotted Road
Deer Park, WA 99006
www.theresemarszalek.com

Published by Word and Spirit Books
P.O. Box 701403
Tulsa, OK 74170

INTRODUCTION

It's no accident that you're holding this devotional book in your hands at this precise moment. Regardless of the avenue through which it arrived, God sent it your way with divine purpose. He heard the cries of your heart, expressed and silent, and is sending the answers you seek, some of which are contained in the pages of this book.

If you feel weary after walking through a long-term wilderness season, I believe you're about to discover hidden treasures in the wilderness that will strengthen you, body, soul and spirit. I encourage you to set time aside during the next 40 days to devote to seeking the treasures God wants to unveil to you. You will not be disappointed!

This 40-day devotional follows on the heels of my most recent book, *From the Wilderness to the Miraculous* (Destiny Image Publishers). If you haven't read it, I hope you'll consider picking up a copy as it lays the groundwork and joins hands in unity with this devotional.

I'm confident that *From the Wilderness to the Miraculous* will change you forever. Through that work, God is breathing resurrection life into areas that wilderness travelers have laid down or let die, and imparting divine revelation of the Father's love.

After emerging from my wilderness season with a greater understanding of the Father's love, the God of love directed me to birth this book in February, which He referred to as "man's month of love." As you pour through the pages of this book, God will pour revelation of His love into your spirit. Man celebrates love in the month of February, but He who *is* love, wants us to celebrate His love *every* day.

Prophetically, the number 40 represents the wilderness. Israel wandered for 40 years in the wilderness after being delivered from the bondage of Egypt. Jesus, after His baptism in the river Jordan, was sent by the Holy Spirit into the wilderness, where for 40 days, He endured intense temptation and testing. You are about to enter yet another 40-day journey.

I never like to see people suffer, especially in the desert where it gets so dreadfully hot and dry. If I had a choice, part of me wishes that those reading *From the Wilderness to the Miraculous* could turn to the last page to find a "Get Out of the Wilderness Free" pass. It would surely become a best seller overnight!

However, knowing the rich rewards that God grants His children as they endure the wilderness, I hope you will complete your personal journey so you don't miss out on His rewards. I have no free pass to give you, but what I do have, I offer to you in Jesus' Name: Encouragement, inspiration and strength—treasures that God imparted to me in the wilderness. May they become riches to you too, as you continue your journey.

40 Days provides the light of God's Word to lead and guide you into all truth. His anointed Word is a lamp to our feet and a light for our path (Psalm 119:105). As you write His Word on the tablet of your heart, it will illuminate that which is in front of you today, and will shine the way for the journey ahead.

Before you begin *40 Days,* I challenge you to purpose to soak in God's presence and meditate on the messages and scriptures each day. Ask God to open your ears to hear what He is speaking to you personally. If you will listen and obey what He reveals, He will enable you to throw off the things that hinder you and will cleanse and rid you of the sin that can so easily trip you up on the journey. With God's Word lighting your path, you can run with perseverance, completing your race in great victory. God himself will be waiting at the finish line to say, "Well done, My good and faithful servant. Enter into your Father's happiness."

As our heavenly Father draws you by His Spirit and transforms you by the power of His Word, may you never be the same again.

DEDICATION

With deep felt gratitude, I dedicate this book to Delsie Duke, treasured daughter of the Most High God. Hand chosen by God as a gift to me, you have impacted my life in more ways than you'll ever know this side of eternity. Selflessly opening your home to me, you provided a haven of peace for me to birth this book in what I will always remember as the Upper Room. Thank you for praying me through what unfolded as the supernatural month of February 2010. Your meals were like manna from heaven to me, and our visits were written on my heart forever. As you enter the last leg of your earthly sojourn with delight and fervor for our wondrous God, I bless you and honor you in Jesus' Name. If you happen to enter glory ahead of me, maybe you can ask God which of His angels has a liking for nuts! I love you, my friend.

DAY 1

MEDITATION

As I fill my heart with God's love, I eliminate available space for fear to take root. On my lifelong journey in Christ, I'm growing daily in my understanding of His love for me. I want to learn my Father's love as He teaches me through His Word and through His personal dealings with me. I submit myself to Him, and insist that fear flee far from me.

May my meditation be pleasing to him, as I rejoice in the LORD.
(Psalm 104:34)

SCRIPTURE FOCUS

Then Jesus said, "Come to me, all of you who are weary
and carry heavy burdens, and I will give you rest."
(Matthew 11:28, NLT)

What is my Father speaking to me through this Scripture?

7

DEVOTION FOR THE DAY

"I have nothing left to give, Lord. *Nothing*," I prayed in desperation. "I'm empty."

Remembering the inexpensive guitar I tried to strum as a young teen, I pictured the twang of strings snapping when I strung them too tight. Feeling as if the strings of my soul had snapped, I couldn't even strum a melody in my heart. "I need to get away *with* You, Father," I continued in prayer. "And I need to get away *from* everything else. Away from distractions, away from phones, away from people."

God heard my plea and started working on my behalf before I had even finished praying.

An unexpected e-mail arrived in my inbox a few days later from Judy Mandeville, a woman who has since become a precious friend. "I have an offer!" the subject line read. Curious, I opened the heaven-sent message.

The Mandeville Manor is available to you as a secret place! You could come here while I'm at work. No phone calls for you. You need to turn off your cell phone. A fire awaits, and a charming atmosphere that can blanket you as you rest and retreat. It's a good offer, dear one. I hope you will embrace the possibility!

Without hesitation, I accepted Judy's most welcomed proposal, a personal invitation orchestrated by a King.

Driving to the Mandeville's home, I sensed the weightiness of the burdens I had been carrying in my heart. Tense muscles crisscrossed my upper back like a roadmap, and then shot through my shoulders. The rest of my body, soul, and spirit, however, felt as if I had been deflated. Like a balloon that had been filled to capacity then pricked by a sharp pin, I had been wildly zooming around in all directions, only to crash when I ran out of air.

Remembering the long-term wilderness season of suffering that I had gloriously emerged from only two years earlier, I said, "Lord God, will I *ever* learn to find the right balance?"

After being miraculously healed, I had hit the floor running instead of staying in step with God's daily plan, my zeal for Him often causing me to spend too much time *doing* for Him and not enough time *being* with Him. My activity level "had runneth over" until I ran dry. I needed a refueling!

Stepping over the threshold of the Mandeville Manor, I entered a serene atmosphere of peace, unlike I had ever experienced in my 49 years. A blazing fire crackled in the fireplace, aromatic candles released a sweet fragrance throughout the house. Soft worship music saturated the air with God's presence, soothing my restless soul.

A place setting of ornate fine china, gold utensils and crystal glasses awaited me in the dining room. Decadent pastries, chocolate swirled cookies, a variety of cheese and crackers and a selection of herbal teas summoned me to a banquet set for a queen.

My inexperience with such elegance made me grin. "What do I do with these tea leaves?" I said, laughing out loud. Seeing the fancy teapot, sugar lumps, tea bags and accessories, I felt unworthy of the feast that my Father, through Judy, had prepared for me. *I don't deserve this,* I thought. But the King of kings, holding out His scepter, beckoned me to His table.

After indulging, I wandered from room to room of the mansion-like home, gazing at the intricate treasures lacing every nook and cranny. In awe of my surroundings, my eyes widened at the keepsakes likely handed down for generations, each with its own story to tell.

I paused in the dining room, eyeing one priceless gem that Judy had shown me earlier. "This one," she had said, "is my favorite." Cupping the once broken wine glass in her hands, she smiled so sweetly as if pondering cherished memories contained in the mended vessel. Seeing a chunk missing in the fragile crystal glass reminded me of my broken life, and the on-going process of God's restoration.

Visiting each room, I spun on tiptoe like a ballerina every once in awhile, knowing nobody was watching. One cozy room seemed to woo me, a chaise lounge opening its arms for me to settle in. I set my bag of

Bibles and study resources aside, wrapped myself in a blanket and snuggled in for the afternoon.

Though I had grandiose plans to pray and study God's Word, I didn't have the strength to even crack a Bible. Instead, I pulled old prayer journals out and began to read of my bittersweet journey with Jesus. Hours later, I picked up my most recent journal and wrote:

> It's been almost two years since I've journaled. Judy Mandeville offered her home as a retreat place for me today. It's heavenly. A fire, candles, waterfalls. It's beautiful. I feel so tightly strung that many layers of stress need to be unwound and unbound so I might relax. In reading my old journals today, I see the magnitude of my weaknesses. I see promises broken and repeated failures. Yet God, in His great love and mercy, never turned His back on me. Though I don't keep my promises, He keeps His. I still struggle with some of the same things as I did long ago. What would God say to me now, in my brokenness and my great sinfulness?

I waited, until God's gentle whisper arose in my heart.

> Do you not know that My love for you is not dependent on you? Do you not know, even by now, that My purpose in you will be fulfilled and is not dependent on you? For I knew you before you were born. I knew this day would come over 49 years later, and I had a plan. Just rest in Me. I will walk with you through everything and I will never leave you or forsake you. You are mine and I set you apart to birth a new day of grace and visitation. My grace covers you, Therese. You are right, you do not deserve it, but My love grants it to you! Just follow Me. Love Me. Love My people. And trust Me. I AM your friend. I AM your God. I AM.

My day at the Mandeville Manor, a divinely orchestrated gift of refreshing and refueling, was the first of many times I responded to the Lord's call to "Come" and find rest in Him. The word "rest," the Greek word *Anapausis*,* means to cease from labor. It implies the relaxing or letting down of chords or strings, which have been strained or drawn tight. Jesus

---

* *Hebrew-Greek Key Word Study Bible*, "Anapausis" (Goodrick-Kohlenberger #398), p. 1586.

beckons us to come to Him, especially in times of weariness when we have been carrying many burdens. If we do our part by coming to Him, especially when we're strung too tight, He will relax our chords and give us rest so we can make a new song in our heart. And He may remind you, as He did me, that His divine plan is not dependent on you.

Whether it's at a Mandeville Manor, or another place chosen by the King, Jesus says, "Come." I AM has an offer for you! As Judy wrote, "It's a good offer, dear one. I hope you will embrace the possibility!"

FOR REFLECTION

I. Schedule at least two hours away with the Lord in a private setting where I will have no disruptions. Be sure to bring a notebook, a pen and an open heart.

2. Reflect on the burdens that weigh on my heart. Make a list of my burdens.

3. One at a time, talk to my Father about the burdens I have been carrying. Release them, one at a time, into His hands.

4. Sit quietly before the Lord and receive His rest. Let Him pour into me, filling me to the fullest capacity.

Reflect on what I am saying, for the Lord will give you insight into all this.
(2 Timothy 2:7)

REPENTANCE

Loving Father, I have taken my relationship with You for granted, turning elsewhere instead of coming to You when I'm weary and burdened. How often I have failed to remember the great price that Your Son paid so that I might come to You. Forgive me for getting sidetracked with the busyness of life and ignoring You when You've summoned me into Your presence. Help me Father, to respond in a way that might be pleasing in Your sight and let me never leave Your presence the same as I arrived.

OTHER AREAS OF REPENTANCE

Repent, then, and turn to God, so that your sins may be wiped out,
that times of refreshing may come from the Lord.
(Acts 3:19)

SUBMISSION

Father God, how I long to be with You. How I long to come away with You for a time of rest and restoration. I offer You my schedules, my agendas and my plans, and ask You to bring divine order to my life, creating regular times of refreshing with You. Lord, I will respond to Your call and will follow where You lead. Here I am, Lord. Have Your way in me. In Jesus' Name.

OTHER AREAS OF SUBMISSION

Submit yourselves, then, to God.
(James 4:7)

FROM THE FATHER'S HEART

My Child, I long to share times of intimacy with you. Even as you sleep, I watch over you and anticipate our next meeting. In the midst of the busyness of your life, I am present and prepared to respond to your every need. Come to Me, My beloved one, give Me your burdens, and I shall give you My rest.

PERSONAL WORD FROM MY FATHER

Speak, LORD, for your servant is listening.
(1 Samuel 3:9)

DAY 2

MEDITATION

Regular times of refreshing are necessary to maintain rest in my soul. Daily, I will respond when Jesus says, "Come." Jesus paid a great price to provide me with the privilege of coming into God's presence so I could give Him my burdens and receive His rest.

May my meditation be pleasing to him, as I rejoice in the LORD.
(Psalm 104:34)

SCRIPTURE FOCUS

There is no fear in love. But perfect love drives out fear,
because fear has to do with punishment.
The one who fears is not made perfect in love.
(1 John 4:18)

What is my Father speaking to me through this Scripture?

_____

_____

_____

DEVOTION FOR THE DAY

"Five, four, three, two, one." On last count, a stage crew woman tapped me on the shoulder and gave me a little push. My stomach fluttered as I stepped down the stairs, then started across the stage at the CBS studio in Hollywood where the Morris Cerullo "Helpline" TV program was being taped.

I was about to meet Dr. Cerullo for the first time, in front of a live studio audience and a television audience of 2.4 billion in 140 nations. Walking toward Dr. Cerullo with open arms, I suddenly realized that although I had entered unfamiliar territory and didn't know what to expect, I was not afraid.

In days gone by, fear accompanied me everywhere. Stalking me most of my life, it first gripped me as a young teen when I lie awake at night wondering what would happen when I died. At times I felt confident that I had earned God's approval and would make it through the pearly gates, but most often, I feared I was destined for hell where dreadful punishment awaited. Not knowing which direction I would go when I took my last breath tormented me daily.

Consuming thoughts of living forever in the flames of Hades vanished one glorious day when I met Jesus. Although I deserved punishment for my sin, I learned that He had taken my place and paid the price for me so that I could be forgiven and live eternally with Him. To this day I'm in awe that a God of love would offer such a gift!

Revelation of God's love drove out the lurking fear of an uncertain eternity. Yet, because my understanding of His love was immature and undeveloped, other fears waited in the wings to haunt me.

In years to come, I confronted fear of flying, fear of man, fear of abandonment, fear of roller coasters and fear of spiders, just to name a few! Yet, as I grew in God's love, those fears melted away, one step at a time and one day at a time. As I embraced God's love, I learned to trust Him, and as I trusted Him, I found rest in Him—in spite of fear producing circumstances. Abiding in God's love produces unwavering trust and rest of heart, and leaves no room for fear!

My daughter Emily, my dear friend Marcia and I once enjoyed a wonderful vacation to Washington, DC, where we traveled around the city by subway. On one of our adventures, when the subway arrived at our stop, we couldn't board the car as it was packed to capacity. Instead of forcing ourselves into the vessel like sardines, we moved on to the next car where we found plenty of room available.

If we're filled to capacity with God's love, *fully persuaded of His unfailing love for us,* fear will find no room available when it tries to hop on board. And if it gets pushy and refuses to settle elsewhere, we can drive it out with God's perfect love.

Our scripture focus says that *perfect* love drives out fear. The Greek translation of the word "perfect" in this verse means *fully mature, full grown, fully developed, perfected, complete, reaching the intended goal, to bring to a perfect state of blessedness and glory so as to win and receive the prize.**

Fear is a big deal to God, who uses many ways of directing us to stay away from it. "Do not fear," "Be not afraid," and "Fear not" are mentioned in scripture about 100 times! Because we are still growing in our understanding of God's love however, we will encounter opportunities to be afraid.

God obviously understood this weakness in man, as He provided the answer for times we face fear. Psalm 56:3 says, "When I am afraid, I will trust in you." That's good news! When you face fear, don't condemn yourself for failing to trust God, but instead, consider it an opportunity to trust Him in spite of your fear! Acknowledge your fear, *then choose to trust Him.*

Because I'm confident of my husband's love for me, I trust him. If Tom told me that pigs were flying out our front window, I would believe

---

* *Hebrew-Greek Key Word Study Bible,* "teleioo" (Goodrick-Kohlenberger #5457), p. 1678

that pigs were indeed flying! I don't believe Tom would intentionally harm me or allow harm to come to me, as he always has my best interest in mind. How much more is God's love for us!

As we grow, mature and develop in our understanding of God's love, we grow, mature and develop in our ability to trust in Him. Trusting our loving Father God will drive fear far from us so we can reach that wondrous place of blessedness, being at a place of perfect rest so as to win and receive the prize.

When the Holy Spirit taps you on the shoulder and says it's time to move, *do not be afraid.* The One giving you a little push, loves you!

FOR REFLECTION

1. Am I confident that my eternity is secure in Christ? On what do I base that confidence?

2. What fears still remain in my life? Make a list of them and talk to the Father about them, allowing adequate time to listen to His personal words to me.

3. Do I believe that God loves me? What hinders me from believing that my Heavenly Father loves me unconditionally?

4. What steps can I take to grow in my understanding of God's love? Do I know any people who appear to abide in the peace of God? Ask them to share their journey with me.

Reflect on what I am saying, for the Lord will give you insight into this.
(2 Timothy 2:7)

REPENTANCE

Holy Father, I have been gripped with fear, which hinders my ability to receive and walk in Your love. I want to be free from fear. Forgive me, Lord, for opening this door for the enemy to come in to steal, kill and destroy. Today, I turn away from fear and turn toward You. Help me, Father God, to receive a greater revelation of Your love for me, that I will overflow with hope and leave no room for fear.

OTHER AREAS OF REPENTANCE

_____

_____

_____

Repent, then, and turn to God, so that your sins may be wiped out,
that times of refreshing may come from the Lord.
(Acts 3:19)

SUBMISSION

I am Your disciple, Father, and I want to be Your student so I can learn from You. I submit myself to You and Your ways of teaching me. I bring my fears to Your altar and ask that You would loose me from fear and enable Your love to be deeply rooted in my heart. Fill me with a greater revelation of Your love for me, that I could walk in perfect peace. In Jesus' Name.

OTHER AREAS OF SUBMISSION

_____

_____

_____

Submit yourselves, then, to God.
(James 4:7)

FROM THE FATHER'S HEART

How I love you, Child of mine. You belong to Me and My love envelopes you daily. I lavish you with My love and pour out My love into your heart by My Holy Spirit. As I pour out My love, pour it out onto others, that I may fill you more. As you grow in My love, fear cannot stand. You will walk in freedom and liberty as you come to full maturity.

PERSONAL WORD FROM MY FATHER

_____

_____

....

Speak, LORD, for your servant is listening.
(1 Samuel 3:9)

DAY 3

MEDITATION

Paul wrote to the Philippians, "I am certain that God, who began the good work within you, will continue his work until it is finally finished on the day when Christ Jesus returns" (Philippians 1:6 NLT). In spite of appearances and regardless of what some might think, God will complete the good work He started in me. God will continue His work in me until He brings it to completion. I must only believe.

May my meditation be pleasing to him, as I rejoice in the LORD.
(Psalm 104:34)

SCRIPTURE FOCUS

"Stop wailing," Jesus said. "She is not dead but asleep."
They laughed at him, knowing that she was dead.
(Luke 8:52b-53)

What is my Father speaking to me through this Scripture?

DEVOTION FOR THE DAY

Jairus, a ruler of the synagogue, was a desperate man. Falling at Jesus' feet, he pleaded for Him to come to his house. His only daughter was dying and Jesus was his last—and only—hope.

Jesus started toward Jairus' home, but was delayed when a desperate woman who had suffered from a 12-year-long bleeding problem, approached Him for healing. Jesus, as He always did when someone sought Him, took time to free the woman from her suffering.

Although he had witnessed a wondrous healing when virtue flowed from Jesus to the woman, Jairus might have sensed growing anxiety at this point. His daughter was near death. They must move on as time was ticking away and every moment counted.

But time ran out. Before they reached their destination where the sick girl was, Jairus received word that his daughter was dead. "There's no reason to bother the Teacher any longer," they told him. His little girl had died and his last hope had died with her.

Yet Jesus, breathing hope into the seemingly hopeless circumstances, told Jairus, "Don't be afraid; just believe, and she will be healed."

I wonder what might have gone through the mourning father's mind. *Just believe? Believe WHAT? My beloved daughter is dead. Her life is over. She isn't breathing. What good is it to believe now?*

Those questions, and more, would surely have gone through my mind too! What good *would* it be for him to believe? The very thought of believing, likely seemed foolish. His precious daughter was gone. It was too late for him to believe and because his daughter had taken her last breath, it was also too late for her to be healed.

Yet Jesus' words, sent forth with divine purpose, would not return void, but would accomplish that which they were sent to accomplish. His life-giving words captured Jairus' heart. *Just believe,* he might have thought, pondering the simplicity of Jesus' words. *Just believe. Jesus, the healer, the miracle worker, told me to just believe.*

As they completed their journey toward his dead daughter, hope emerged and faith took hold, preparing Jairus for the scene he would encounter back home, where people were already mourning and wailing his daughter's death.

Jesus, unmoved by the thick atmosphere of death, told the mourners, "Stop wailing! She is not dead, but asleep."

It's understandable why people laughed when Jesus claimed that the girl was merely asleep. She was no longer breathing; her body was already cool. Rigor mortis had likely set in. All signs in the natural realm indicated that Jairus' daughter was, in fact, dead. Funeral plans were already underway. She needed burial.

But Jesus, speaking resurrection life to the little girl, said, "My child, get up!" At once, her spirit returned and she stood up. Imagine Jairus' response when his little girl arose! When all seemed hopeless, Jesus breathed resurrection life into his family.

Has someone sent word that the things for which you've believed God, have died? Have people advised that it's no use praying or asking God for help any longer, as it's too late? Are funeral plans already underway to bury and forget your God given dreams?

"Just believe," Jesus says. "Just believe." People may laugh, as they laughed at Jesus, when you proclaim that life remains in that which appears dead. As you profess, "It's not dead, but asleep," you likely will not receive applause or standing ovation. "Aw, come on!" some may mock in unbelief. "It's too late for that dream. Forget about it. Can't you see, it's...dead?!"

As Jesus said to Jairus, don't be afraid; just believe. Take Jesus to the place where rigor mortis appears to have set in, even if the wailing and mourning over the death of your dream is drowning out your confession of faith. *Just believe*. Let faith take hold and capture your heart. *Just believe*.

Hold fast to that which God has conceived in you. In spite of appearances, it's never too late with Jesus. Death itself cannot survive when He breathes resurrection life into that which is dead or appears dead. Nothing is impossible with a God of love, who *will* bring to completion and birth that which He conceived in you.

The dreams God planted in your heart may be asleep at the moment for one reason or another—maybe even due to your own error or misjudgment—but Jesus is here to breathe resurrection life into that which is dead. Receive His breath of life by faith, and allow God to set in motion the manifestation of that which He designed and destined for your life.

Don't be afraid. *Just believe*.

FOR REFLECTION

1. What promises has God given me, personally and through His Word, for which I've been standing?

2. Have any of God's promises appeared to have died an early death? Explain.

3. What have people told me about the promises God has given me? Who has encouraged me? Who has discouraged me?

4. My Father says, "Don't be afraid. Just believe." What does this statement mean to me?

Reflect on what I am saying, for the Lord will give you insight into all this.
(2 Timothy 2:7)

REPENTANCE

Merciful Father, I'm sorry for the times I've listened to and believed those who have wailed over the death of the promises and dreams You've given me. Forgive me for my lack of belief while I focused on appearances. Wash away my sin of unbelief, Lord, and help me become strong in faith.

OTHER AREAS OF REPENTANCE

_____

_____

_____

*Repent, then, and turn to God, so that your sins may be wiped out,
that times of refreshing may come from the Lord.*
(Acts 3:19)

SUBMISSION

Most High God, I give You, again, all of which You have entrusted me. I thank You for the good work You've started in me and I trust that You will continue it until You complete that work. I will cooperate with You and Your plan, and will continue to believe Your promises in spite of my circumstances or appearances. In Jesus' Name.

OTHER AREAS OF SUBMISSION

_____

_____

_____

Submit yourselves, then, to God.
(James 4:7)

FROM THE FATHER'S HEART

I rejoice in your renewed trust in Me! The dreams I have given you will surely come to pass. The good work I've started in you, I will bring to completion. Everything will happen according to My flawless plan and perfect timing. Be not afraid! Just believe. For you will see resurrection life in that which others have said is dead, and I shall be glorified in and through it.

PERSONAL WORD FROM MY FATHER

Speak, LORD, for your servant is listening.
(1 Samuel 3:9)

DAY 4

MEDITATION

My feelings, which are vulnerable and can change like the wind, do not determine my identity. God's Word, the unshakeable, immoveable, unchanging truth, determines who I am. In spite of how I feel, God's Word is the only truth I shall stand on. When the accuser of the brethren brings his lies, I will prevail as I choose to stand on God's truth.

May my meditation be pleasing to him, as I rejoice in the LORD.
(Psalm 104:34)

SCRIPTURE FOCUS

For the accuser of our brothers and sisters has been thrown down
to earth-the one who accuses them before our God day and night.
And they have defeated him by the blood of the Lamb and by their testimony.
(Revelation 12:10-11, NLT)

What is my Father speaking to me through this Scripture?

_____

_____

_____

DEVOTION FOR THE DAY

While preparing for an upcoming ministry activity, a black cloud of despair crept in and settled over my mind like a demonic halo. Timing for a torrential spiritual storm was not good. Not only was I scheduled to minister at Women Aglow in Coeur d'Alene, Idaho, and Destiny Church in Spokane, I would also appear that week on the "Testimony of Jesus" television program and a television crew had arranged to tape preliminary footage at my home for the Morris Cerullo "Helpline" TV program.

The sudden ominous cloud enveloped me so unexpectedly that I didn't realize what had hit me until the storm was well underway, and I missed the spiritual signs flashing "THIS IS ONLY A TEST!"

Caught off guard in a time of weakness, I became entwined in Satan's lies and accusations, which brought an overwhelming sense of hopelessness and worthlessness. Instead of standing on the truth of God's Word regarding my identity in Christ as I often wrote or spoke of with confidence, I became ensnared in the devil's trap, coming into agreement with his lies and feeling condemned for mistakes of the past. I wondered if I was even saved!

In the midst of the storm, I wrote in my prayer journal:

I hate myself. I hate my life. I'm full of despair, I'm sad and grief stricken. I'm bitter and I'm angry. There is no good thing in me. Not one. If not for Jesus who lives in me, I would be completely worthless. I feel sorry for Jesus, as He has to live in me. I imagine if He could, He would leave too. How do I end my despair? Nobody, not one, understands. And I am to minister life to others? What a mockery! I will somehow fulfill my ministry commitments in the next weeks, but then I quit. What was I thinking? To think I could bring others hope when I have none myself. If I could only find a way to end this suffering. How often I've asked God to deliver me, only to find myself here again. He can't help me or deliver me because I'm not even worthy to be delivered. And I am to teach others of God's love when I myself, am unworthy of His love? Everyone, especially my family, would have been much better off without me. How can I be God's representative like this? I can't. What do you want from me, God? I serve You, yet You won't deliver me. I've done all I know to do, yet You allow me to be tormented day and night. I'm too weak to do anything. I've asked You for help, yet You just leave me here to suffer. Why didn't You just let me die, so my suffering would end? I don't blame You for abandoning me, as I would abandon myself if I could. I hurt so badly and I see no way out.

The enemy had left his fingerprint in the storm. Yet God, in His loving mercy and grace, found me in the pit of darkness, and breathed hope into my hopelessness. As if He had given me heavenly smelling salts, I received God's breath of life. Spiritually resuscitated, I started coming to my senses. A few days later, I wrote:

Although I feel despair, I repent of coming into agreement with the enemy's lies. I resist his lies in Jesus' Name and come into alignment with the truth of Your Word, Lord. Pull me from the pit of torment, God. Please help me! Please send help, God.

With God's help, my grief, like King David's laments, turned to praise:

I have the victory in Christ and the enemy is defeated again. My arsenal has been made ready. Lord, give me wisdom, lead me to the tools I need. Put a determination in my heart to choose the right road. And may I always stay in agreement with You, God, the unchanging truth. Thank you Jesus! I praise You, God, for delivering me from the pit. Lord, lead and direct as I follow. Teach me what I need to learn. I submit to Your training, Father, help me to learn, O God, and help me gather the tools You have provided to better prepare for that which You have created me. My trust is in You!

Resisting the enemy's lies and coming into agreement with the truth of God's Word smashed the demonic oppression and caused the spiritual storm to lift. Accomplishing more than I had asked or imagined through ministry endeavors the following week, God sent my testimony of His grace to the ends of the earth for His glory.

Believing and agreeing with Satan's lies brings severe consequences, giving momentum to a destructive path that gives us amnesia about our true identity in Christ. *In Christ,* you are who God says you are. *In Christ,* you are victorious. *In Christ,* you are forgiven by the blood of the Lamb. That's the truth!

When Satan leaves his fingerprint in a storm of accusations and lies, stay in agreement with the truth! As you stay the course, even through the storms, God will turn your test into a test*imony*. If the accuser of the brethren reminds you of your past, remind him of his future in the eternal lake of fire! Satan *is* defeated by the blood of the Lamb and by the word of your testimony.

FOR REFLECTION

1. With my heart open before God, what do I believe about my identity? I believe these things about myself:

2. In reviewing the above list, are my beliefs in agreement with what God says about me? Are my beliefs the truth or are they lies of the enemy?

3. Study and document five scriptures regarding my identity in Christ. Ask my Father to lead me to those scriptures that will address areas of weakness in me.

4. Verbalize the scriptures documented in question #3 daily. Write them on sticky notes and display them where I will see them regularly. Memorize them and speak them aloud daily.

Reflect on what I am saying, for the Lord will give you insight into all this.
(2 Timothy 2:7)

REPENTANCE

O God, maker of heaven and earth, I come to You on bended knee. Forgive me, Lord God, for coming into agreement with the lies of the enemy and for wavering in my faith in You and Your Word. May Your Word be established in my life and my heart, directing me on the path of truth and righteousness.

OTHER AREAS OF REPENTANCE

_____

_____

_____

Repent, then, and turn to God, so that your sins may be wiped out,
that times of refreshing may come from the Lord.
(Acts 3:19)

SUBMISSION

I surrender my mind to You, Lord. Your Word is truth, O God, and I desire for Your truth to light my path all of the days of my life. Make me aware of the snares of the enemy when he comes with lies that contradict Your Word. When his flaming arrows come, I will lift my shield of faith. In Jesus' Name.

OTHER AREAS OF SUBMISSION

_____

_____

_____

Submit yourselves, then, to God.
(James 4:7)

FROM THE FATHER'S HEART

My little lamb, I shall lead you always and will search for you when you go astray. You can trust Me to lead you to green pastures where you will find abundant life that I desire for you. My love for you is unfailing; I will never lead you on the wrong path. I am with you, even in the midst of the storm. After the storm, My Child, My rainbow comes. Without the storm, there can be no rainbow. Without the darkness of the night, the light of the day cannot arise. I am with you always, even to the end of the age.

PERSONAL WORD FROM MY FATHER

_____

_____

_____

Speak, LORD, for your servant is listening.
(1 Samuel 3:9)

DAY 5

MEDITATION

It is my choice to trust God or to trust my circumstances. If I choose to trust Him, and put my confidence in Him, I can dwell in perfect peace. I cannot keep myself in perfect peace, only God can. But in order for Him to keep me in peace, I must do my part by trusting Him and His Word and putting my confidence in Him and His Word. I choose today to trust God.

May my meditation be pleasing to him, as I rejoice in the LORD.
(Psalm 104:34)

SCRIPTURE FOCUS

You will keep in perfect peace all who trust in you,
all whose thoughts are fixed on you!
(Isaiah 26:3, NLT)

What is my Father speaking to me through this Scripture?

_____

_____

_____

DEVOTION FOR THE DAY

The prophet Jeremiah shares a good news/bad news situation: "But blessed are those who trust in the LORD and have made the LORD their hope and confidence. They are like trees planted along a riverbank, with roots that reach deep into the water. Such trees are not bothered by the heat or worried by long months of drought. Their leaves stay green, and they never stop producing fruit" (Jeremiah 17:7-8, NLT).

First the bad news: Trial laden seasons of scorching heat and famine-like drought *will* visit our lives. That news flash shouldn't come as a surprise to followers of Christ, as God provided advance notice that they would face afflictions—*many* afflictions! (Psalm 34:19.) Even while we're in right standing with God through faith in Christ, doing everything we know to do, we will face trials of *many* kinds.

Now the good news! If we keep our hope and confidence in God, which are the natural results of trusting God, we will be blessed as we walk through the heat and drought—and we can remain worry free and fear of free in the process! When trust is present, faith abounds to eradicate worry and fear. As faith drives those enemies out, we can be fruitful in spite of circumstances that heat us up or dry us out!

Putting our trust and confidence in anything or anyone other than the one true God sets us up for a fight with fear and a battle with worry. In the midst of that battlefield, God may send another grace-laced news flash to help us grow: *If you're plagued with worry and fear, you're not trusting Me!*

Choosing to trust God in spite of circumstances positions us for God's best. Isaiah 26:3 says, "You will keep in perfect peace all who trust in you, all whose thoughts are fixed on you!" (Isaiah 26:3, NLT).

Keep means "to be hidden, guarded, watched, and protected." *Peace* means "peace, safety, prosperity, well-being, wholeness and completeness."* Therefore God will hide us in, guard us with, watch over us, and

---

* *Hebrew-Greek Key Word Study Bible,* "nasar" (Goodrick-Kohlenberger #5915), p. 1535 and "salom" (Goodrick-Kohlenberger #8934), p.1557

protect us with His perfect peace, safety, prosperity, well-being, whole-ness and completeness, IF our mind is stayed on Him because we trust in Him and put our hope in Him. What rich benefits to trusting God!

I know a remarkable man who reminds me of Jesus, as he consis-tently exudes the peace of Christ. After Charles and his wife had raised their children, they adopted a special needs baby who had been born to a drug addicted mother. Together this loving couple helped Baby Carlos through drug withdrawal, then started their journey of parent-ing. With patient endurance and love, they learned to work with the longer-term challenges left behind as a consequence of the biological mother's drug use during pregnancy. Years later, Charles lost his beloved wife to cancer and was left to raise their son alone while himself facing several physical afflictions.

Although Charles faces daily challenges, you'd never know it. With a cheerful attitude, he not only takes on his personal challenges willingly and with a smile, but he always seems to be on the lookout for opportu-nities to bring joy to others. And God, no doubt, takes notice!

Charles had eye surgery recently to correct complications from diabetes. After returning home to recover, he took a serious fall, crack-ing part of his spine. His tumble sent him back to the hospital and then to long term nursing care to face more physical suffering. Yet when I visited him, I didn't hear even one complaint. This humble servant gives praise to God in the midst of his pain, pouring out a heart of gratitude for God's goodness. What a role model for all of us! Instead of getting bitter at God for his circumstances, Charles chooses to get better! When life's circumstances squeeze Charles, God's life comes out.

This man after God's own heart has discovered hidden treasure in the dark places. The level of peace in which Charles walks is the fruit of putting his trust and confidence in God *in spite of* difficult circumstances. Charles is clothed in God's peace because he keeps his eyes focused on Jesus—and he is able to focus on Jesus because he trusts Him.

When the heat rises and the pressure gauge spins out of control, our carnal mind strives to evaluate circumstances with our natural eyes, instead of with the eyes of faith. The eyes of faith focus on God, trusting Him and His Word *regardless of circumstances—even if nothing makes sense.* God and His Word can and will change our circumstances, but our circumstances will never change God or His Word.

If you've lost your peace or if fear and worry are tormenting you through a prolonged drought or rising heat, take your eyes off of your circumstances and fix your gaze upon Jesus. Putting your trust and confidence in Him promises to be a fruitful endeavor!

FOR REFLECTION

1. What does "perfect peace" mean to me? How would I rate myself on the issue of peace?

2. *Peace* literally means "peace, safety, prosperity, well-being, wholeness and completeness." Recite Isaiah 26:3, inserting each of these words in place of the word *peace.*

3. What tangible ways can I grow and mature in the areas mentioned in #2?

4. Whose responsibility is it to keep me in perfect peace? Whose responsibility is it to trust God and put my confidence in Him? Are they dependent on each other?

Reflect on what I am saying, for the Lord will give you insight into all this.
(2 Timothy 2:7)

REPENTANCE

Dear God, how I have grieved You by my lack of trust in You. Forgive me, O Lord, for I have sinned. I'm sorry for the ways in which I've forsaken You and Your Word, instead choosing to put my trust in what I see or feel. How I need your peace, Lord, and how I need Your help in growing to full maturity in peace as I trust in You.

OTHER AREAS OF REPENTANCE

_____

_____

_____

Repent, then, and turn to God, so that your sins may be wiped out,
that times of refreshing may come from the Lord.
(Acts 3:19)

SUBMISSION

Father, I know that Your ways are not my ways. You know what is best for me and You know the ways in which I learn best. I submit to Your training, Lord, and ask that You would help me to learn to trust You and put my confidence in You in a greater measure. In Jesus' Name.

OTHER AREAS OF SUBMISSION

_____

_____

_____

Submit yourselves, then, to God.
(James 4:7)

FROM THE FATHER'S HEART

Dear One, how I delight when you come before Me like a child. How I delight when you trust Me and take Me at My Word, following Me wherever I lead. I shall take you by the hand and lead you to a deeper place of trust. Come, follow Me. We will walk together all the days of your life.

PERSONAL WORD FROM MY FATHER

Speak, LORD, for your servant is listening.
(1 Samuel 3:9)

DAY 6

MEDITATION

God says that I can do all things through Him who strengthens me. Without Him, I can do nothing, I can change nothing, I can achieve nothing and I can overcome nothing. But through Him, and by His Spirit, I am an overcomer! Daily, I will receive His strength and daily I will overcome.

May my meditation be pleasing to him, as I rejoice in the LORD.
(Psalm 104:34)

SCRIPTURE FOCUS

I tell you the truth, unless a kernel of wheat falls to
the ground and dies, it remains only a single seed.
But if it dies, it produces many seeds.
(John 12:24)

What is my Father speaking to me through this Scripture?

DEVOTION FOR THE DAY

"I'm in the process of dying," I told the cashier after she greeted me and asked how I was doing.

"What?" She stopped ringing up my grocery items, her wide eyes searching for an explanation.

I was indeed in the process of dying. Dying to self. Dying to my flesh. Dying to having my own way so I could live God's way. I longed to obtain what the apostle Paul shared in his letter to the Galatians, to be crucified with Christ, that I would no longer live, but Christ would live within me (Galatians 2:20).

My death had been a slow, grueling process. Approaching God's altar, I often presented my body a living sacrifice, asking Him to make me holy and acceptable to Him. The problem was, I kept crawling off the altar! My strong-willed self, instead of surrendering to its crucifixion, rallied and determined to remain very much alive.

When the shrill alarm rouses me from a sound sleep at 5 am, self wants to turn over and snooze several more hours instead of planting my feet on the floor and heading to my prayer time. When it's time to exercise, self pitches a fit. Although needing to remain strong and physically fit to accomplish what God asks of me, self votes to pass on physical activity, preferring instead to lounge on the couch with a good book and a steaming cup of java. Instead of maintaining a healthy balanced diet, self lusts after several helpings of gooey chocolate deserts and mouth-watering pastries. When opportunities arise to extend grace and forgiveness to those who knowingly or unknowingly do me harm, self muscles in, jockeying for its self-righteous position. And the list goes on.

Finding abundant life in Christ requires mortifying the flesh-self, and can be like trying to tame a wild stallion. The flesh-self, unlike the spiritual-self, is a spoiled brat who is used to having its way. Self doesn't want to surrender any comfort and staunchly resists anything requiring effort or self control. Self turns its nose up at sacrifice of any sort.

The flesh-self and the spirit-self that dwells within, conflict with one another continuously, daily duking it out for dominance. If the spirit does not rule, the flesh bullies self around, stomping its feet and demanding its selfish way.

The Apostle Paul explains the conflict between the spirit and the sinful natured self: "So I say, let the Holy Spirit guide your lives. Then you won't be doing what your sinful nature craves. The sinful nature wants to do evil, which is just the opposite of what the Spirit wants. And the Spirit gives us desires that are the opposite of what the sinful nature desires. These two forces are constantly fighting each other, so you are not free to carry out your good intentions" (Galatians 5:16-17, NLT).

The sinful nature and fleshly desires do not miraculously disappear after we invite Christ to dwell in our hearts. Although the spirit was reborn and made new, the flesh-self remains and is determined to live and not die. Yet flesh-self, like a kernel of wheat, must die in order for us to live the abundant life God desires for us.

Dave White, a fourth generation wheat farmer in St. John, Washington, shared the amazing life cycle of wheat with me, reminding me of my impending death to self.

Although at first hidden from the human eye, when a kernel falls to the ground it develops new life within, converting starch into sugar to feed itself. Within a week, it sprouts roots that start absorbing water and nutrients from the soil, while at the same time nutrients from its original shell run out.

The kernel must give up everything it has ever known to take on its new life. The transformed seed, producing a sprout that reaches toward the sun as it grows, produces other seeds that will also bring life. Those new seeds, when developed, will fall to the ground and start the process all over again.

Like the kernel of wheat, those who belong to Christ Jesus must die, crucifying the sinful nature with its passion and desires (Galatians 5:24).

We, like the seed, must surrender everything we've known to take on new life in Christ. As we continue dying to self, giving up our ways and receiving nourishment from the Son instead of from self, Christ lives through us, radiating His glory and bringing life to others.

Dying to self is a daily, lifelong process. The flesh-self, always ready and willing to take the reins, needs a constant reminder that the spirit, not the flesh, is in control and that it *will* do things God's way, not its way.

By enlisting the help of the Holy Spirit, the spirit-self will rule and reign in victory! Then we, like the grain of wheat that falls to the ground a single seed, but dies and produces many, will produce a great harvest from which others can feed.

As the cashier continued ringing up my groceries, she glanced at me, still in search of a response. Realizing how shocking my words of an impending death must have sounded, I spoke up. "Oh, it's not what you think," I said with a smile. "I've never been better!" Dying to flesh-self brings life!

FOR REFLECTION

1. What areas of my life have yet to be surrendered to God?

2. Thinking of the areas mentioned above, how have I tried in my own strength to conquer them? Am I struggling in the flesh, or have I allowed God to work through me as an overcomer? Have I worked by my might, by my power, or by God's Spirit?

3. In what areas of my life has God already enabled me to find victory? How did I overcome in those areas?

4. Am I prepared to surrender all to my Father, allowing Him to live through me and strengthen me by His Spirit?

Reflect on what I am saying, for the Lord will give you insight into all this.
(2 Timothy 2:7)

REPENTANCE

Heavenly Father, giver of life, forgive my futile efforts to overcome struggles in my own strength. I'm broken; I'm at the end of myself. I acknowledge the error of my ways, O God, and know I can do nothing without You, but can do everything through You. I desire to correct the error of my ways, Lord, and to walk fully in Your ways.

OTHER AREAS OF REPENTANCE

Repent, then, and turn to God, so that your sins may be wiped out,
that times of refreshing may come from the Lord.
(Acts 3:19)

SUBMISSION

Loving Father, I bring You my many failed attempts to change. I've tried to do things my way, but now surrender all to You and Your ways. I need Your help. May Your will, and not my will, be done, O God. I give You my body, soul and spirit, and ask that You make me more like You. I'm dependent on You for all, Lord God, and willingly give You my life. In Jesus' Name.

OTHER AREAS OF SUBMISSION

....

....

....

Submit yourselves, then, to God.
(James 4:7)

FROM THE FATHER'S HEART

Do not be afraid. For what you consider an ending is a beginning to Me, and in a beginning, I will do new things. Out of your brokenness, I will bring beauty. Out of death, I will bring life. Time is short and there is much for you to do. Do not be afraid, My child. For I, the Lord, am with you.

PERSONAL WORD FROM MY FATHER

....

....

....

Speak, LORD, for your servant is listening.
(1 Samuel 3:9)

DAY 7

MEDITATION

Satan, the accuser, uses a hellacious megaphone to bring accusations against me. I will no longer allow him to have a voice of influence. When the enemy condemns me, my Father writes on my heart, "I Love You!" I am forgiven because I AM forgave me. Because of the shed blood of Jesus, my sin has been washed away and I stand before my Father white as snow. Because I am forgiven and free from the shame of my past, I can hold my head high, knowing I'm a child of the Most High God.

May my meditation be pleasing to him, as I rejoice in the LORD.
(Psalm 104:34)

SCRIPTURE FOCUS

"Then neither do I condemn you," Jesus declared.
"Go now and leave your life of sin."
(John 8:11)

What is my Father speaking to me through this Scripture?

DEVOTION FOR THE DAY

Imagine the distressing scene. People had gathered around Jesus as He taught in the temple courts. A sudden interruption erupted when Pharisees and teachers of the law brought a woman caught in the act of adultery, her sin exposed for all to see, drawing piercing stares from surrounding spectators. Cringing from their silent judgment, she recoiled from the sting of shame. Downcast and knowing her sin deserved punishment, her heart raced as she awaited judgment. She had, after all, broken one of God's top 10 commands!

Forcing her to stand before the group, the adulterer's accusers reminded Jesus that according to the Law of Moses, this scorned woman must be stoned (Leviticus 20:10, Deuteronomy 22:22-24). Challenging Jesus, they asked what ought to be done with this shameful sinner. With arms crossed over their prideful chests, they awaited His reply, hoping to trap Him into saying something they could use against Him.

Jesus, aware of what they were doing, stooped down and wrote in the ground with His finger. If He contradicted the Law of Moses, they could condemn Him as a false prophet. Yet, if He sentenced the woman to death, they could accuse Him of usurping Roman authority.

After His accusers questioned Him further, Jesus stood up. "If any one of you is without sin," He said, "let him be the first to throw a stone at her." (John 8:7.) Then stooping down again, He went back to his writing. The Bible doesn't tell us what Jesus wrote, but I wonder if He made an X in the sand, silently putting His finger on each one's individual sin as they searched their conscience with stone in hand.

One by one the woman's accusers and witnesses left, the older first, until only Jesus stood with her. None could condemn her. None were without sin.

Jesus, the only One without sin, didn't condemn her either. Yet He drew the line—it was time to leave her sin behind. Pointing the woman in the direction that would lead her to a new life, He declared, "Go now and leave your life of sin" (John 8:11).

Just as the Pharisees dragged the woman before Jesus, Satan, the accuser of the brethren, drags us before the throne of God where Jesus sits at the right hand of the Father. While Jesus makes intercession on our behalf, the accuser announces our sin with his hellacious megaphone, "Look!" he taunts, "I caught them in the act!"

Wagging his blaming finger, Satan shames God's children. "Your followers disobey and compromise Your commands! They have no self-control! They rob you by withholding their tithe! They refuse to forgive! They abuse their bodies!" Satan's personal accusations are many, and new ones pop up daily.

Satan is right about one thing: We *are* sinners. And our sins are *many*. Big or small, hidden or exposed, obvious or subtle, sin is sin. And sin must be judged.

In a spiritual court of law, the sentence would follow. Satan's verdict: "Guilty! Stone her! Sentence him to death!" But God, a God of love, a God of justice, offers us grace when we repent. His verdict: "Because My only begotten Son paid the penalty for their sin, I'm giving them a pardon! They're free to go!"

Only through Jesus can we receive God's pardon and be freed from the eternal punishment we deserve for our sin. Out of His unfailing love, Jesus willingly left His heavenly dwelling and came to earth to save us. Although we reap natural consequences for our choice to sin, if we repent and accept the gift of Jesus as Savior, our slate of sin—which proves our guilt and demands our punishment—is wiped clean.

God is drawing the line in the sand *today*. Examine your heart and respond in repentance to the areas God is putting His finger on and marking with an *X*. He's been patient and long suffering, but today He says, "I love you. *Go now, and leave your life of sin.*"

FOR REFLECTION

1. In what areas of my life can I relate to the woman caught in adultery? Does anything from my past cause me to feel shame or condemnation? Explain.

2. Have I ever sensed man's judgment toward me? If so, how has this judgment affected me?

3. Come before the Father with a humble heart. Tell Him about the situations where I felt judged or condemned and ask Him if He judges me. What was His response?

4. Does anything from my past seem to haunt me on a regular basis? I will examine my heart for areas in need of repentance. Do I need to repent of unforgiveness toward those who have judged or condemned me? Forgiveness is available for me right now. I will confess my sin to my Father and be washed clean.

Reflect on what I am saying, for the Lord will give you insight into all this.
(2 Timothy 2:7)

REPENTANCE

Father of compassion, forgive me for allowing unconfessed sin to remain in my life. Forgive me for neglecting to receive Your gift of forgiveness. Though I hang my head in shame, I know You are the lifter of my head. Help me, O God, to respond to You when You put Your finger on areas I need to change. I come before You with a repentant heart today, and ask that You wash away my sin once again. As I leave my life of sin, help me to turn my life in a new direction.

OTHER AREAS OF REPENTANCE

Repent, then, and turn to God, so that your sins may be wiped out,
that times of refreshing may come from the Lord.
(Acts 3:19)

SUBMISSION

O God, though I have sinned against You, You have welcomed me into Your arms of grace and mercy, embracing me with your unfailing love. I'm grateful, Father, for Your patience with me as You awaited my return. I want to honor You in and through my life, Holy Lord, and I ask that You take me and make me what You created me to be in You. In Jesus' Name.

OTHER AREAS OF SUBMISSION

Submit yourselves, then, to God.
(James 4:7)

FROM THE FATHER'S HEART

I do not accuse you, My precious child. I embrace You today, and welcome You into My arms. I will never leave you or forsake you, even when you feel you have failed Me. I welcome you today with open arms, My love, and will always welcome you with open arms. I AM the God of love. I AM love and I will never change. You are mine and nobody can snatch you out of My mighty hand. You, little One, I have written on the palm of My righteous right hand.

PERSONAL WORD FROM MY FATHER

Speak, LORD, for your servant is listening.
(1 Samuel 3:9)

DAY 8

MEDITATION

My Father has a good plan for my life and has given me everything I need for life and godliness through my knowledge of Him who called me by His own glory and goodness. He provided me with His written Word as a roadmap to lead me and guide me through life. As I follow His plan, and stay within His established boundaries, He will cause me to prosper and live life to the fullest.

May my meditation be pleasing to him, as I rejoice in the LORD.
(Psalm 104:34)

SCRIPTURE FOCUS

This day I call heaven and earth as witnesses against you
that I have set before you life and death, blessings and curses.
Now choose life, so that you and your children may live.
(Deuteronomy 30:19)

What is my Father speaking to me through this Scripture?

_____

_____

_____

DEVOTION FOR THE DAY

"I can't believe it!" my husband mumbled when he returned from his morning walk with our yellow Lab. "Cars run that stop sign at the corner every day!"

Tom continued to vent. "Some people don't even glance either way before plowing through the *obvious* stop sign," he huffed. "And others run the intersection when nobody's coming from the other direction."

The real clinker came one morning when Tom pointed at the stop sign as one habitual lawbreaker approached the intersection. The speeder shot Tom an ear-to-ear grin, then belligerently raced through the intersection.

Suspecting Tom may have embellished his story a bit, I started taking note of the happenings at this intersection. He was right. The majority of cars blew through the intersection without a care. Businessmen, teenagers and Moms alike, were seemingly blind to the fact that a red octagon with the letters "S-T-O-P" on it means the driver should stop, *then* proceed if it's safe to do so.

Our neighborhood is no different from other neighborhoods across suburbia. Citizens break the law.

Citizens of heaven break God's spiritual laws, too.

Peppered throughout God's written Word are what could be considered rules and regulations. God provided boundaries, not because He is a hard taskmaster, but because He knows what is best for us and wants us to enjoy the abundant life He promises.

God commands us to resist adultery (Exodus 20:14). Obeying His command creates a faithful, committed marriage that thrives with joy, happiness and intimacy. Disobeying His command by committing adultery, however, leads to broken families, wounded children and shattered lives.

God commands us to love one another (John 13:34). Obeying this command with a love-filled life births the bonds of unity, peace and righteousness. Disobeying this command through a loveless life, however, entangles us in bitterness, unforgiveness and hatred; all snares of the enemy that steal God's blessings.

And the list goes on. Deuteronomy 28 lists 21 blessings that will be yours "if you obey the Lord your God." Those blessings of obedience, however, are followed by an even lengthier list of curses that will come upon you "if you refuse to listen to the Lord your God." The blessings of the Lord are not automatic. Our choice to obey or disobey God's ways determines the degree to which we walk in His blessings.

Like the stop sign near our home, God sets His clearly established rules for our good, yet many arrive at the crossroads of obedience and, without a second thought, disregard Biblical instruction. Instead they choose compromise, obeying only regulations that are comfortable, unrestrictive, or witnessed by others.

As a young mother, I used to leave my cart in the parking lot after loading my groceries in the car. I realized one day that my inconsideration could result in damage to another car if a gust of wind slammed my abandoned cart into a parked car, not to mention that someone else would eventually have to return my cart to its appropriate place.

That day I purposed to return my cart to its right spot, whether it's pouring rain or if the cart storage is on the other side of the parking lot. Whether or not I return my cart might seem insignificant, but because God brought it to my attention, it's highly significant. God takes notice every time I return my cart and I know He's pleased. He sees *everything* we do.

Once after a heated debate with my husband, I begrudgingly gave in on a decision I had rallied against. I guarded my mouth from spewing out what I wanted to express, yet marched upstairs, slammed the bedroom door, and grumbled under my breath to my heart's content. A sudden awareness that God had witnessed my tantrum brought me to my knees. God hears *everything* we say.

Just as some run stop signs when nobody is present, some cross the boundaries set in God's Word, thinking their actions went unnoticed. "Nothing in all creation is hidden from God. Everything is naked and exposed before his eyes, and he is the one to whom we are accountable" (Hebrews 4:13, NLT).

What we may consider a minor compromise or act of disobedience hinders us from receiving God's fullness. Although His grace covers our ignorance, as we grow in spiritual maturity and learn what God expects of us, we become accountable to Him and cannot claim ignorance.

Though many run stop signs seemingly without consequence, eventually we will reap the consequences of our obedience or disobedience to God's commands. As long as the earth endures, God's law of sowing and reaping (seedtime and harvest) will never cease; just as cold and heat, summer and winter, and day and night will never cease (Genesis 8:22). It's God's law!

Ignoring God's Word creates blind spots that can cause unexpected collisions on our Christian journey. When God puts a spiritual "STOP" before you, slow to a complete stop and heed His warning; *then* proceed when it is safe to do so.

FOR REFLECTION

1. What yellow caution lights has God put in my path to warn me to use extreme caution when I proceed? Have I heeded God's warnings? What was the result?

2. What stoplights has God put in my life? Did I stop and seek His direction or did I run the stoplight? What was the consequence of my choice?

3. As I reflect on the yellow and red lights God has put in my path, do I sense any guilt or condemnation for the times I may have disobeyed God's laws? Explain.

4. Set some time aside to bask in God's presence. Turn my cell phone and computer off and talk to my Father about the experiences shared above. What have I learned?

Reflect on what I am saying, for the Lord will give you insight into all this.
(2 Timothy 2:7)

REPENTANCE

Lord of my life, here I am again with sin-stained hands asking Your forgiveness provided through Your blood-stained hands. I have knowingly strayed outside Your boundaries and chosen to go my own stubborn way. I've ignored the warning signals and stops You've put in my path. I'm sorry for my wrong attitude that surfaces when I suffer the consequences of my wrong choices. Help me, Lord, to become more like You.

OTHER AREAS OF REPENTANCE

_____

_____

_____

Repent, then, and turn to God, so that your sins may be wiped out,
that times of refreshing may come from the Lord.
(Acts 3:19)

SUBMISSION

God of all comfort, Father of compassion, here I am again, submitting myself to You. Thank You for welcoming me again, and for Your willingness to take my hand and lead me again, even when I've been unfaithful. I submit myself to Your plan, O God, and ask You to fill me with knowledge of Your will where my life is concerned. Give me eyes to recognize Your warnings and give me a heart of obedience to heed those warnings so You will be glorified through my life. In Jesus' Name.

OTHER AREAS OF SUBMISSION

Submit yourselves, then, to God.
(James 4:7)

FROM THE FATHER'S HEART

Come now, My child, and I will show you the way. For you are like a little child and must learn the boundaries I have established for your life. Many dangers of which you are unaware lurk outside the boundaries, to steal, kill and destroy. I have come to bring you life and life abundantly! Trust Me and know that the warning signals and red lights I have put in your path are there for your good and for My glory.

40 DAYS

PERSONAL WORD FROM MY FATHER

_____

_____

_____

Speak, LORD, for your servant is listening.
(1 Samuel 3:9)

DAY 9

MEDITATION

My thoughts today will impact my actions tomorrow, and my actions today will impact my thoughts tomorrow. I can choose what I allow myself to meditate on and can choose to resist wrong thoughts, taking them captive and making them obedient to Christ.

May my meditation be pleasing to him, as I rejoice in the LORD.
(Psalm 104:34)

SCRIPTURE FOCUS

Whatever is true, whatever is noble, whatever is right,
whatever is pure, whatever is lovely, whatever is admirable—
if anything is excellent or praiseworthy—think about such things.
(Philippians 4:8)

What is my Father speaking to me through this Scripture?

DEVOTION FOR THE DAY

I've had it.

Once again my inbox is full of unwanted e-mail messages. Just today these unsolicited communications offered me the opportunity to refinance a mortgage I don't have, purchase life insurance I don't need, and lose 10 pounds overnight—though I don't have 10 pounds to lose. A popular matchmaking company wants to introduce me to the perfect mate, yet I'm already happily married to the man of my dreams! Not a few e-mails promise big earnings if I'll start a home business, for which I don't have time and if I'm willing to pull out my credit card, I can snap up countless e-deals for a wide variety of items for which I have no need.

Before I can focus much needed attention on the personal messages that I need and want, I'm forced to first wade through and delete these bothersome e-messages that have invaded my inbox like so many uninvited guests. It irritates me to waste valuable time on something for which I didn't ask!

Responding to my expressed frustrations, my computer savvy husband ran a virus check, then ensured that my laptop's spam filter had been upgraded and was fully engaged. What a nifty invention! After recognizing and seizing unwanted e-mail messages, the filter then redirects them to a spam file, which I can delete with a flick of a keystroke. No longer wasting time on these e-irritants, I capture them, then send them to their demise before even giving them a glance.

Unwanted thoughts can arrive as some e-mails arrive—unannounced and uninvited. Negative, judgmental, and critical thoughts can unexpectedly slip into our mind's inbox and can steal more than valuable time. Some of these bothersome thoughts—*you're a loser, you're a failure, God will never forgive you*—come sneaking in to contradict God's Word regarding our blood bought identity in Christ. Other inappropriate thoughts can also pop in with no advance warning and leave us wondering, "Where did THAT come from?"

Thoughts are not sin. Although we can't control all thoughts that enter our mind, we can determine our response to those thoughts. If we don't take appropriate action by giving them the boot, evil thoughts sown by the enemy can *lead to sin.*

When the enemy knocks on our door saying, "You've got mail!" we have a choice to make. If he delivers adulterous thoughts for example, we can open the door, offer a warm welcome, invite them in, entertain them and invite them to stay as our guest. If that guest is allowed to remain, that thought of adultery can eventually develop into the act—and sin—of adultery. People don't wake up one day and decide to commit adultery. The sin of adultery starts as a thought and is entertained long before the action is played out. It's a choice.

The better choice is to engage our thought filter! Second Corinthians 10:5 tells us to "demolish arguments and every pretension that sets itself up against the knowledge of God," and to "take captive every thought to make it obedient to Christ." We can choose to capture those thoughts, send them to the trash bin and press the "delete" key!

A fine tuned thought filter is developed through prayer, study of God's Word and filling up on Philippians 4:8—"Whatever is true, whatever is noble, whatever is right, whatever is pure, whatever is lovely, whatever is admirable-if anything is excellent or praiseworthy-think about such things."

A heart and mind full of God-thoughts leaves little room for uninvited evil thoughts that might try to drop in. And if they do arrive unannounced, we'll be prepared to show them the door or take them captive and put them in the trash bin, where they belong.

You've got mail! Is your thought filter engaged today?

FOR REFLECTION

1. As I evaluate my thought life, on what have my thoughts been focused? Have past emotional wounds consumed my thoughts? What thoughts do I need to take captive and make obedient to Christ?

2. Reflecting on the thoughts mentioned above, find several scriptures that I can use when destructive thoughts drop in unannounced.

3. Schedule a fast from wrong thoughts and trust my Father for the duration of the fast. When the enemy sends unwanted thoughts into my "inbox," choose to resist them, posting a sign that reads, *No Trespassing! God's Property!*

4. When I arise in the morning, consciously think about what is on my mind and choose to set my course with the right thoughts.

Reflect on what I am saying, for the Lord will give you insight into all this.
(2 Timothy 2:7)

REPENTANCE

God and Father of my Lord Jesus, forgive me for allowing my mind to be the devil's playground. I'm sorry for the ways in which I've allowed wrong thoughts to dominate my mind, and for entertaining that which dishonors You. Forgive me, Lord, for sin that has resulted from an unrestrained thought life. Help me, O God, to purify my thought life and to post my *No Trespassing! God's Property!* sign when ungodly thoughts arrive unannounced.

OTHER AREAS OF REPENTANCE

_____

_____

_____

Repent, then, and turn to God, so that your sins may be wiped out,
that times of refreshing may come from the Lord.
(Acts 3:19)

SUBMISSION

I give You my thought life today, Father God. Fill me with Your thoughts, fill me with Your ideas, fill my mind with that which will honor You. Make my mind a place where Your Spirit wants to dwell. Take hold of my thoughts as You take hold of my heart. Help me to recognize wrong thoughts and resist them instantly. In Jesus' Name.

OTHER AREAS OF SUBMISSION

_____

_____

_____

Submit yourselves, then, to God.
(James 4:7)

FROM THE FATHER'S HEART

My cherished one, how I long to fill your body, soul and spirit with thoughts of Me. How I long for you to dwell in Me and My Word. As you hunger and thirst for Me, I shall fill you to overflowing. As You come near to Me, I come near to You. As you think on Me, I will release a sweet fragrance in your thoughts that will follow you wherever you go.

PERSONAL WORD FROM MY FATHER

Speak, LORD, for your servant is listening.
(1 Samuel 3:9)

DAY 10

MEDITATION

The devil has no authority over me. God has authority over the devil and has given me His authority to stand against him. When I submit myself to God and resist the devil, he must flee. I have no reason to fear the devil, as Jesus defeated him at the cross. As I remain in Christ, no weapon the devil forms against me can prosper.

May my meditation be pleasing to him, as I rejoice in the LORD.
(Psalm 104:34)

SCRIPTURE FOCUS

Be self-controlled and alert. Your enemy the devil prowls around
like a roaring lion looking for someone to devour.
(1 Peter 5:8)

What is my Father speaking to me through this Scripture?

DEVOTION FOR THE DAY

I must have been an easy target.

While Tom and the kids were away for the week at youth camp, I stayed back to hold down the fort. Life was good! I had cleared my schedule so I could enjoy having the entire house to myself in peace and quiet. My only commitment was to care for and walk our dogs.

Early one morning, with Gracie, my three pound Yorkie on one leash and Harley Anne, our 60 pound golden retriever puppy on the other leash, we headed out the front door for our daily stroll. Although I normally followed the same route through the neighborhood, today I decided to take an unfamiliar route.

While the day's planned activities raced through my mind, I drank in the crisp morning air. Enjoying the brisk walk, I paid no attention to my surroundings as I ventured into a neighborhood with which I was unfamiliar.

All was well, until we turned a corner to discover a muscular pit bull bounding around a house, headed straight toward us. His black and brown streaked hair stood up on its spine like an army of well-trained soldiers. As he skidded to a halt on the sidewalk in front of us, we had no choice but to halt too. The frightening canine became statuesque, stiffened and poised to take on all three of us at once. His aggressive stance seemed to invite a fight, warning us that we had crossed the boundaries into his territory.

Seeing the monstrous pit bull eye Gracie's tiny tail wiggling to and fro, shivers shot up my spine. Knowing this sharp-toothed animal could gobble my Gracie in one easy gulp, I squatted in slow motion to scoop up my little lap dog, unwilling to see her become a living sacrifice. Trying to avoid eye contact with the pit bull's black beady eyes, I straightened up, still in slow motion. Then I became like a statue, frozen with fear.

Much to my dismay, Harley Anne, who is normally skittish and cowers behind me if a dog of any size comes near, suddenly was free from all fear. Eager to get a good whiff of the dog, Harley tugged hard, pulling toward the pit.

Not now, Harley!, I screamed in silent thought. As Harley sniffed the fearless canine, it growled through snarled teeth. My heart pounded in my chest, sure that our Harley would soon be minced meat.

Images flashed on the screen of my memory bank of the dog attack reports I had heard over the years. I had seen pictures of young children who had been seriously injured and animals needlessly killed by aggressive dogs. Gripped with thoughts of being this animal's next victims, I knew we needed rescue.

"Jesus," I said under my breath.

After what seemed like an eternity, the owner came out his front door with a high-pitched whistle. Eying me one last time, the dog spun around and galloped around the corner where he came from.

Still frozen in position, clutching Gracie to my chest, I shook off the fear, unknotted my stomach, and exhaled as I made a beeline for home. I never took that route again.

Like the pit bull, the enemy comes prowling, on the lookout for an opportunity to devour with a surprise attack, paying particular attention to those who venture into territory with which they are unfamiliar. Especially if that territory is *his* territory.

But if we stay on the path God set before us which leads to life, staying the course in spite of obstacles, we need not fear when the enemy seems to appear from nowhere to intimidate, scare and manipulate.

If we're on the right path, we can stand our ground, posting a sign that reads: *No Trespassing! God's Property!* And if we knowingly or unknowingly venture off course and run into trouble, we can call on the Name that is above every name. Jesus, our ever-present help in times of trouble, is only a prayer away and always offers a plan for rescue.

FOR REFLECTION

1. As I ponder my journey with Jesus and the path I've walked with Him since the beginning, think of a time I may have strayed off the path into enemy territory. Explain.

2. What obstacles did I encounter when I ventured into unfamiliar territory?

3. Did I call on God for help? If not, why didn't I call on Him? How was I rescued and redirected onto the right path?

4. Am I afraid of the devil? Explain. Look up Luke 10:19, James 4:7 and Colossians 2:15 and meditate on these scriptures and memorize them.

Reflect on what I am saying,
for the Lord will give you insight into all this.
(2 Timothy 2:7)

REPENTANCE

Loving Father, forgive me for the times I've strayed away from You and ventured into enemy territory. I want to learn from the error of my ways, Lord, so I might become better equipped for what is ahead. I'm sorry for running in fear from the devil instead of standing in the authority You have given me. O God, I need You.

OTHER AREAS OF REPENTANCE

_____

_____

_____

Repent, then, and turn to God, so that your sins may be wiped out,
that times of refreshing may come from the Lord.
(Acts 3:19)

SUBMISSION

I come under the shadow of Your wing, Father. I desire to follow the path of righteousness You have set for me through Your Holy Word. Help me stay on the right path, O God, that I might not sin against You. Increase my understanding of the authority You have provided for me through the shed blood of Your Son, that I might walk in that authority wherever You send me. In Jesus' Name.

OTHER AREAS OF SUBMISSION

_____

_____

_____

Submit yourselves, then, to God.
(James 4:7)

FROM THE FATHER'S HEART

My beloved, I am with you always, even when you stray off the path. Wherever you are, My precious one, turn to Me now. If you have wandered, turn back to Me where you are safe. My angels are round about you. I guard your path, My child, and protect your way. Do you not

know that I look after the lilies in the fields and the sparrows in the air? How much more do I care about and watch over you. Do not fear, for no one can snatch you out of My hand. You are sealed by My Spirit for all of eternity.

PERSONAL WORD FROM MY FATHER

_____

_____

_____

Speak, LORD, for your servant is listening.
(1 Samuel 3:9)

DAY 11

MEDITATION

I am pregnant with divine purpose! As the Holy Spirit has overshadowed me, I have conceived a spiritual pregnancy and with great delight I receive that which God is developing within me. He will walk me through the development, preparation and labor. This spiritual baby will be born for God's glory!

May my meditation be pleasing to him, as I rejoice in the LORD.
(Psalm 104:34)

SCRIPTURE FOCUS

The thief comes only to steal and kill and destroy;
I have come that they may have life, and have it to the full.
(John 10:10)

What is my Father speaking to me through this Scripture?

DEVOTION FOR THE DAY

The dream seemed so real. I sat on a metal exam table in the doctor's office, waiting for him to finish reviewing my medical report. "You're pregnant," he said without looking up, "but your baby is dead." Shaking his head, he added, "We need to abort right away." His emotionless countenance chilled the already frigid exam room.

Flipping my chart shut, he turned and left without another word, closing the door hard as if inserting an exclamation point to his grave report. Alone, I reeled from the news of an unexpected pregnancy, and I wept, grieved at the thought of losing my baby.

A ray of warmth shone through the exam room when a cheerful nurse appeared. Dressed in a whiter-than-white uniform, as nurses dressed long ago, she glowed from the top of her bleached cap to the soles of her snowy polished shoes.

Beaming, she glanced at her clipboard, then smiled at me with a twinkle in her eyes. Overflowing with joy, she started rattling off instructions. "You must eat lots of fruits and vegetables," she said with delight. "Get adequate protein, remember to take your vitamins, and it's important to get plenty of exercise." Hardly able to contain her exuberance, she continued providing precise directions for a healthy pregnancy.

Confused by her instructions, I interrupted. "Why are you telling me these things? Don't you know?" I pleaded. "My baby is *dead!* There is no pregnancy!"

"Oh, no!" she said with glee. "Your baby is *not* dead. You surely *are* pregnant and you surely *will* give birth to this baby!"

God, the Giver of Life, has news for you today! You're pregnant with His divine purpose!

Satan, the spiritual abortionist, has heard the report of your pregnancy too, and wants to steal, kill and destroy that which God has conceived in you.

Trying to convince God's children that their spiritual pregnancies are dead, Satan comes with his grave report. "It's time to abort! It's time to quit!" he says, "God's purpose for your life is dead!" Devising schemes to abort God's purpose, even while we're young, he strives especially to snuff out God's plan while it's in the early stages—before you're showing evidence of the wondrous life developing within.

As I shared in my book *Extraordinary Miracles in the Lives of Ordinary People*, part of God's purpose for me was to speak publicly. Although being in front of any size group terrified me, God didn't hesitate to create opportunities for me to remain in the public eye. And every time, I suffered intense fear.

In God's perfect time, He revealed the enemy's scheme: a stronghold of fear that had taken root in a ninth grade social studies class, then haunted me for 30 more years. Although the enemy designed this scheme to abort God's plan, God revealed it, then set me free from it. Our loving God doesn't want us to be ignorant of the enemy's schemes! He wants us to come full term and birth that which He conceived in our spiritual womb.

If Satan fails to abort God's plan during the term of our spiritual pregnancy, he often comes in like a flood, bringing intense trials right before the birth. Like natural pregnancy, we will face our greatest pain when we go into labor. Although the pain can seem overpowering, this isn't the time to quit. *This is the time to push!*

While giving birth to James, my first son, it amazed me that women would even consider having more children! That was labor talk though, an attitude that changed as soon as James arrived. Cradling him in my arms and looking into his big brown Bambi eyes, I didn't dwell on the labor pain I had just endured, I marveled at the fruit of my labor!

If you're reeling after getting news that you're pregnant with purpose, know that something very special is being developed within. In spite of the enemy's feeble attempts to steal, kill and destroy, God will indeed enable you to come full term to birth that which He is forming in you.

If you've had a prolonged, difficult labor and are tempted to quit, don't do it. Instead, *PUSH!* Press through this temporary season. When you see the fruit of God's purpose unfold, you will marvel at His goodness and the labor pains you suffered will become a faint memory.

FOR REFLECTION

1. For what purpose do I believe God put me on the earth? Did I receive God's plan or have I distanced myself from it? Ponder the relation between physical pregnancy and spiritual pregnancy. Do I believe I am pregnant with purpose?

2. Has anyone told me that I would never accomplish what I believed God wanted me to do? Explain. What impact did this have on the way I viewed my calling?

3. Can I identify schemes of the devil to abort the plan for which God designed me? Explain.

4. What stage of my spiritual pregnancy am I currently experiencing? Am I in the developmental stage or is it time for me to push through labor?

Reflect on what I am saying, for the Lord will give you insight into all this.
(2 Timothy 2:7)

REPENTANCE

Father God, Creator of heaven and earth, as I humble myself and examine my life, I recognize that I have failed in so many ways. Though

You have equipped me with divine purpose, I have often doubted it would ever come to pass. I've listened to the lies of the enemy and believed I was unworthy to be used of You in such amazing ways. I'm sorry, Lord God, that as I've doubted myself, I've really been doubting You. I'm sorry, Father. Forgive me for my sin.

OTHER AREAS OF REPENTANCE

_____

_____

_____

Repent, then, and turn to God, so that your sins may be wiped out,
that times of refreshing may come from the Lord.
(Acts 3:19)

SUBMISSION

O God, I leap and jump for joy at the news of my spiritual pregnancy! I embrace You now and I embrace what You are developing within me. I receive my callings with gratitude and submit myself to the path You have set before me in preparation for birth. I love You, Father, and though I don't know exactly what this spiritual baby will look like, I trust You to develop it according to Your perfect plan. I'm honored, Lord, to serve You. In Jesus' Name.

OTHER AREAS OF SUBMISSION

_____

_____

_____

Submit yourselves, then, to God.
(James 4:7)

FROM THE FATHER'S HEART

Dearly beloved, you are My chosen vessel to birth My purpose. Do not despise the preparation and growth stages of what I am developing, as all are necessary and critical. Embrace Me as you embrace My purpose. You will give birth at just the right time and all will marvel at what I have done in and through you. I'm a proud Daddy!

PERSONAL WORD FROM MY FATHER

_____

_____

Speak, LORD, for your servant is listening.
(1 Samuel 3:9)

DAY 12

MEDITATION

Jesus was always about His Father's business, doing only what the Father wanted Him to do. At times He even walked past people who were sick. Following His example, I will live a fruitful life if I ask for and receive direction from my Father before I commit to new activity.

May my meditation be pleasing to him,
as I rejoice in the LORD.
(Psalm 104:34)

SCRIPTURE FOCUS

Be still before the LORD and wait patiently for him.
(Psalm 37:7)

What is my Father speaking to me through this Scripture?

_____

_____

_____

DEVOTION FOR THE DAY

"Don't just stand there. *Do something!*" Many hear this command when mounting pressure from all sides demands us to jump into premature action. If the strain doesn't ease up, we feel compelled to do something. *Anything.* At the height of other people's expectations, before we're prepared to make a move, before we know which direction we're supposed to go, we do something. And often regret it later.

Our fast paced world of e-mail, texting, drive-throughs and instant messaging, pushes us to be on the go, filling every moment with continuous activity. Because multiple needs and crises put our abilities in high demand, we can easily be headed in too many directions at the same time. And if we ignore God's "Disaster Ahead" warning signals, we eventually head for a collision course where we—and often those around us—crash and burn.

I once saw an impressive juggling act that left an imprint on my heart. With precise movement, the juggler handled multiple balls, knives and fire in the air with perfection. One wrong move, one item out of place, would create a disaster that would bring the curtain down.

Likewise, struggling to juggle too many activities can make our worst nightmares become a reality. If one activity turns up in the wrong place at the wrong time, we lose our balance, sending everything else spinning out of control.

If we don't regain our balance, the vicious cycle continues, splitting families, frazzling our emotions and turning healthy relationships into dysfunctional relationships.

Frantic and unable to rearrange our lives into proper formation, guilt and self-condemnation plague us. Failing to meet everyone's expectations as a perceived super-Christian, we become painfully aware that we didn't check off every item on our bulging "To Do" list, couldn't serve on every committee, and were unable to be everything to everyone. When we're overloaded and lose our peace, physical, emotional and spiritual exhaustion often set in.

God never expected us to be involved in every activity, to serve on every committee, or to fill every job opening. Performance drive was not God's plan. He has a better game plan.

While the world screams, "Don't just stand there, *do* something!" God says, "Don't just do something, *stand there!*" Consider putting the brakes on your activity overload and allow yourself to touch base with the One who ordained your steps with exact precision and perfect timing.

Ephesians 2:10 says that we are God's workmanship, created in Christ Jesus to do good works, which God prepared in advance for us to do. God designed the plan for our entire life before we were born, and ordained—in advance—certain works for us to accomplish during our earthly sojourn.

Staying in tune to God's plan and responding as He leads, enables us to walk through every activity blanketed in His peace. His perfect plan equips us with the ability and strength with which to accomplish everything He calls us to do.

For the God-orchestrated game plan, we must first seek our Heavenly Coach for wisdom and guidance, then stand still until He reveals the plays. Man's agendas and pressures of the world push us to run our own plays or mistakenly launch into activities without consulting God first. Time spent in prayer will not only equip you with the best plan but will strengthen your endurance to withstand the influential pressures trying to lure you into activities for which God did not design you.

Invitations will come to serve in various capacities. It's ok to pray about it! Even if some interpret your desire to pray as an excuse to decline, take time to pray. God wants you to ask Him for the game plan. When the Coach gives the go-ahead, a seasoned team player willingly accepts the position and when the Coach says, "No, this isn't part of My plan for you," a team player declines without suffering needless guilt or condemnation. A Hall of God's Fame team player is more interested in following the Head Coach's plan than in the approval from well-meaning people shouting flawed plays from the sidelines.

Psalm 37:7 says, "Be still before the LORD and wait patiently." Being still means to be silent, be quiet, become deaf, say nothing and make no moves until Coach Jesus gives the go ahead—even if every fan in the stands is pressuring you to make a move *now*.

The phrase "wait patiently" is from the Hebrew word *chul* and means to stay self, set self to expect an answer. Be determined to expect an answer.*

Instead of filling every free moment with activity, come to Jesus first and ask Him what He's planned in advance for you to do. Then, don't just do something—stand there until He reveals the next play to accomplish His divine plan.

FOR REFLECTION

1. Examine and document my current schedule of activities. Which activities are fruitful and which ones lack fruitfulness? Which activities bring me inner joy and which ones cause inner turmoil?

2. Reflecting on each activity listed in #1, did I pursue God's wisdom and direction before committing to this activity? Explain.

3. When needs arise, personally, spiritually and professionally, do I jump in to meet the need or do I prayerfully consider if it's something with which I should become involved? Do I know how to say "no"?

---

* *Dakes Annotated Reference Bible,* "chul" (item [i]), p.564

4. Set time aside to review my schedule with my Father and ask Him for divine guidance on possible adjustments to my commitments. When I receive His direction, prune what does not belong that I might become more fruitful.

Reflect on what I am saying, for the Lord will give you insight into all this.
(2 Timothy 2:7)

REPENTANCE

Father of compassion, I've mucked up my life with so much activity that my time with You is often squeezed out. I'm sorry, O God! Fear of man has driven me into commitments I should not have made. Forgive me for caving in to the pressures and expectations of man instead of looking to You for direction. Help me, Lord God, I want to do what is pleasing in Your sight.

OTHER AREAS OF REPENTANCE

Repent, then, and turn to God, so that your sins may be wiped out,
that times of refreshing may come from the Lord.
(Acts 3:19)

SUBMISSION

Lord God, I bring my schedule, my plans and my agenda to Your altar. I surrender all to You and invite You to help me prune my sched-ule. Cut out anything that is not part of Your divine plan. I give You permission to make necessary changes so I can be more fruitful for Your kingdom. In Jesus' Name.

OTHER AREAS OF SUBMISSION

_____

_____

_____

Submit yourselves, then, to God.
(James 4:7)

FROM THE FATHER'S HEART

I have ordained your steps, treasured one, and have a wondrous plan for every season of your life. I delight when You come to Me for direction and marvel at the joy you experience when You fulfill the works for which I've created you. I hold the answers you need. I have the wisdom you need and I have the keys you need to unlock the door of My divinely orchestrated plan. Ask and you will receive.

PERSONAL WORD FROM MY FATHER

_____

_____

_____

Speak, LORD, for your servant is listening.
(1 Samuel 3:9)

DAY 13

MEDITATION

While Jesus hung on the cross with the sin of the world nailed through His hands and feet, He said, "My God, My God, why have You forsaken Me?" Jesus understands my feelings of abandonment and knows how it feels to be seemingly forgotten. But God hadn't forgotten Him, and He hasn't forgotten me! Though He seems far away, He is so close that He can feel the breath from my nostrils.

May my meditation be pleasing to him, as I rejoice in the LORD.
(Psalm 104:34)

SCRIPTURE FOCUS

But God remembered Noah and all the wild animals and the livestock that were with him in the ark, and he sent a wind over the earth, and the waters receded.
(Genesis 8:1)

What is my Father speaking to me through this Scripture?

_____

_____

_____

DEVOTION FOR THE DAY

Does it appear as if God has forgotten you? You're in good company if it does. When I experienced a five-year season of suffering and uncertainty, heaven become like brass. I cried out for help, but only the echo of my voice bounced back like a well seasoned boomerang. I knew God was omnipresent, being everywhere at the same time, but it seemed as if He had somehow forgotten my address! It felt as if I had been left to fend for myself, remembered no more by my Creator.

Appearances and feelings, however, are deceiving and perceptions can go askew, especially if you happen to be walking through a long-term season of trial. Though it can seem as if we have been long forgotten in our greatest time of need, *God remembers*.

God did not forget Noah when destruction was about to come upon every creature. Warning Noah in advance, God directed him to build the ark, and said that the rains would pour down and wipe out every living thing on the earth.

It came to pass, just as God said. For 40 days and 40 nights, torrential rains fell and the floodwaters grew deeper, covering the ground and lifting the boat 22 feet above the highest peaks. Yet while the floods brought death to every living thing, the ark which God had directed Noah to build, floated safely on the surface.

Imagine how overwhelming it might have been for Noah to peek out the window after being shut in the ark for 40 days with his family and two of every animal, discovering water as far as his eye could see in every direction. Yet Noah had nothing to worry about because *God remembered*.

Genesis 8:1 says, "*God remembered* Noah and all the wild animals and the livestock that were with him in the ark, and he sent a wind over the earth, and the waters receded." Twelve and a half long months after the flood began, the earth dried out and Noah, his family and their animal friends were able to leave the ark so they could be fruitful, multiply and fill the earth as God had directed.

God did not forget Abraham or his nephew Lot when He prepared to rain down fire and burning sulfur from the sky, utterly destroying Sodom and Gomorrah where Lot lived. The fiery destruction wiped out all the people and every bit of vegetation (Genesis 19:24-25). But *God remembered* Abraham (v. 29) and delivered Lot and his relatives to safety before devastation came.

God did not forget Rachel, Jacob's wife, who cried out to God in desperation as she longed for a child. "*God remembered* Rachel; he listened to her and opened her womb" (Genesis 30:22). When God remembered her, she brought forth Joseph, who would save Israel from severe famine, and his brother Benjamin, two of twelve leaders of the tribes of Israel.

God did not forget Hannah. Beloved wife of Elkanah, Hannah was distressed because her womb was also closed. But *the Lord remembered* her (1 Samuel 1:19) and she became pregnant and gave birth to Samuel, one of the great Old Testament prophets.

It is to our benefit to remember what God wants us to remember and forget what He wants us to forget. We seem to more easily remember what He wants us to forget and forget what He wants us to remember.

God remembers us, and when we repent, He forgets our sin. Because He remembered us, He forgets our sin. *He remembered* us in our weaknesses, His faithful love endures forever (Psalm 136:23, NLT), and He says, "I, even I, am he who blots out your transgressions, for my own sake, and remembers your sins no more" (Isaiah 43:25). If you've confessed your sin, God has forgiven and forgotten.

Don't forget, in spite of how it appears and regardless of how you might feel, God has not forgotten you. He will *never* forget you. But remember, as He remembered His people since the beginning of time, *He remembers you!* You're carved on the palm of His hands.

FOR REFLECTION

1. Have I ever felt as if God had forgotten about me or didn't care about my suffering? Have I ever felt like an abandoned orphan? Explain.

2. At the time, how did I respond to feeling as if God had forgotten or abandoned me? Was I angry with Him? Did I feel rejected?

3. Reflecting on previous seasons of apparent abandonment, how did God respond to me during that time? In looking back, where can I see His hand reaching into my loneliness?

4. Set some time aside to talk to my Father about the times I shared above. Tell Him how I felt as I walked through seasons when I felt abandoned, then listen. What is He saying to me?

Reflect on what I am saying, for the Lord will give you insight into all this.
(2 Timothy 2:7)

REPENTANCE

My Lord and my Savior, I fall on my knees in repentance before You. You promised to never leave me or forsake me, yet at times I've believed a lie that You had forgotten me. I'm sorry, Father, for questioning Your presence in my life. I'm sorry, Father, for putting my faith in my feelings instead of in You. Cleanse me, God, wash me clean again, O God.

OTHER AREAS OF REPENTANCE

_____

_____

_____

Repent, then, and turn to God, so that your sins may be wiped out,
that times of refreshing may come from the Lord.
(Acts 3:19)

SUBMISSION

Father God, Lord of my life, I bow my heart before You and surrender every circumstance of my life to You. Teach me, God, to be ever aware of Your presence, even when it feels like You're not there. Even if everyone else abandons me, I know You will never abandon me. With heart lifted high, I shall walk with You. I shall talk with You and I shall remain one with You all the days of my life. In Jesus' Name.

OTHER AREAS OF SUBMISSION

_____

_____

_____

Submit yourselves, then, to God.
(James 4:7)

FROM THE FATHER'S HEART

When everyone seems to have forgotten you, I remember you. When your enemies rise up against you, I remember you. When you feel alone and discouraged, I remember you. Even when you are in sin, I remember you. When the walls seem to be closing in on you and it

seems as if you will never emerge from the wilderness, I remember you. My child, you are always on My mind. I have never missed even one second of your life. I will never, ever leave you or forsake you.

PERSONAL WORD FROM MY FATHER

Speak, LORD, for your servant is listening.
(1 Samuel 3:9)

DAY 14

MEDITATION

I have no need to hide anything about myself from my loving Father. He already knows every detail about me and loves me right where I am, character flaws and all. Instead of denying my dire need for change, I will acknowledge the truth of who I am and submit myself to God so He can give me a new name. I will stay in the ring and wrestle with God until His purpose is fulfilled in me.

May my meditation be pleasing to him, as I rejoice in the LORD
(Psalm 104:34)

SCRIPTURE FOCUS

"What is your name?" the man asked. He replied, "Jacob."
(Genesis 32:27, NLT)

What is my Father speaking to me through this Scripture?

DEVOTION FOR THE DAY

"The 'H' is silent," I'd tell Mrs. Falk, my fourth grade teacher, every time she pronounced my name incorrectly.

"It's not THer-eese, it's Ter-eese," I'd correct her politely. My frustration grew throughout that schoolyear, as Mrs. Falk never did get my name right. At times I wished I could choose a new, easier name, wondering if my parents might have been better off naming me "Claire" as they had considered.

Jacob, son of Isaac and Rebekah, needed a new name, not because anyone mispronounced it, but because he needed a new identity.

A wrestler, Jacob had his first rough and tumble match with his twin brother Esau while still in their mother's womb. Living up to his name, which means "heel catcher, supplanter, schemer and deceiver," Jacob was sneaky. Taking advantage of his brother at a weak moment of hunger, he cheated Esau out of his birthright for some stew. And, with his mother's help, he deceived his father Isaac, stealing the blessings intended for the firstborn, Esau.

Everything changed one night when Jacob came face to face with God in an all-night wrestling match. Jacob, who had strived to obtain God's blessing throughout his life by deceiving and conniving others to get what didn't belong to him, now was determined to face God and prevail in obtaining His blessing the right way.

When daybreak came, the match had to come to a close. Yet when the Lord told Jacob to let Him go, Jacob wouldn't let go. "I won't let go until you bless me!" he said. (Genesis 32:26.) This desperate, yet tenacious man, held fast as he wanted God to change him.

Knowing Jacob was still in a stronghold, the Lord asked him, "What is your name?" God, of course, knew Jacob's name, but wanted Jacob to admit his current identity before God could give him a *new* identity.

"Jacob," he answered the Lord, acknowledging his character identity as a heel catcher and deceiver.

"Your name will no longer be Jacob," God told him. "From now on you will be called Israel, because you have fought with God and with men and have won." Jacob, known as a deceiver, now had a new, God given identity. Jacob had fought with God and won, now God would fight for him.

Jacob didn't walk away from that wrestling match unscathed. With an injured hip, he now walked with limp, a reminder that trying to obtain God's blessings in his own strength would no longer suffice. As He continued His life journey, though many lessons still awaited him, he would now walk with a greater dependence on His God.

Are you wrestling with character issues? Maybe you need a name change.

What is *your name?* What character trait identifies you? Can you take off your mask, humble yourself and acknowledge to God who you really are? If you'll admit your identity to Him, He will change your identity *in Him.*

If you're in an all-night wrestling match with God right now, don't let go, even if you see the break of dawn! Be tenacious like Jacob, and hold on until God changes you. You will still have much learning ahead, but you will walk in a greater dependence on the God who has written your name in the Book of Life (Revelation 13:8), the God of Abraham, Isaac and Jacob.

FOR REFLECTION

1. Humble myself before the Lord and acknowledge my character strengths and character flaws. List them now.

2. What areas of my character have I wanted to change but not yet found success? What has hindered me from changing?

3. What adjustments will become necessary if I allow God to change my character flaws? Will my environment need to change? Will the people with whom I surround myself need to change?

4. Set some time aside to get quiet before God. "What is your name?" He asks. Tell my Father about myself, who I am and what I want to change. If led, get in the ring with God for a wrestling match and don't let go until He changes me.

Reflect on what I am saying, for the Lord will give you insight into all this.
(2 Timothy 2:7)

REPENTANCE

Holy and righteous God, You are perfect, without flaw, yet I am imperfect and flawed in so many ways. I've strived to change myself in my own strength and have found no success. I have failed to renew my mind with Your Word to bring transformation to my life. Give me a greater hunger for You, Your Word and Your righteousness, God. I'm holding on to You and won't let go until You bless me.

OTHER AREAS OF REPENTANCE

_____

_____

_____

Repent, then, and turn to God, so that your sins may be wiped out,
that times of refreshing may come from the Lord.
(Acts 3:19)

SUBMISSION

Father, I want a new name. I willingly enter a wrestling match with You and want You to take me to the mat. Pin me to the floor, God. Do whatever You need to do in me so that I might be changed into the image of Your Son, Jesus. Transform my character to reflect your beauty. Here I am, O Lord, do whatever You need to do to change me into the person You created me to be. In Jesus' Name.

OTHER AREAS OF SUBMISSION

Submit yourselves, then, to God.
(James 4:7)

FROM THE FATHER'S HEART

Child of Mine, I named you while you were being formed in your mother's womb. I knew you from the beginning and delight in watching you grow. I called you by name and appointed you to lift My Name in the earth. Submit yourself to Me daily, surrender all to Me. As we walk together, I will change you, prune you, and love you into the person I created you to be in Me. Just walk with Me. Just *be* in Me. I will change you from the inside out and even you will marvel at the work of My hand.

PERSONAL WORD FROM MY FATHER

Speak, LORD, for your servant is listening.
(1 Samuel 3:9)

DAY 15

MEDITATION

God's goodness leads me to repent. When the conviction of the Holy Spirit helps me recognize my sin, I can respond in repentance so He can lead me in a new direction. Condemnation is from the enemy, not from God. As I acknowledge my sin before God, He will strengthen me to do an about face and will lead me by the hand in a new direction that leads to His abundant life.

May my meditation be pleasing to him, as I rejoice in the LORD.
(Psalm 104:34)

SCRIPTURE FOCUS

*If my people, who are called by my name, will humble themselves
and pray and seek my face and turn from their wicked ways, then will
I hear from heaven and will forgive their sin and will heal their land.*
(2 Chronicles: 7:14)

What is my Father speaking to me through this Scripture?

_____

_____

_____

DEVOTION FOR THE DAY

"Left. Your left. Your left, right left." A well-trained platoon leader barks this commands to his unit, keeping them in perfect synch. As he calls cadence, the soldiers listen to and follow his commands, marching in unity and staying in step with their fellow comrades. When the commander issues an About Face, the seasoned soldiers reverse direction and continue marching in the opposite direction.

With two children and generations that have gone before us who served in the military, marching to cadence has been the subject of many family stories. My husband says that an About Face usually led to lots of smirks, grins and sometimes outright laughter, albeit short lived because it usually ticked off the Drill Instructors! Sometimes, when a soldier was asked to step forward out of ranks, then given an About Face to return, they spun completely around, doing a 360 instead of a 180, like a ballerina doing a pirouette!

Repentance, like the cadence call, is an About Face, a complete change of direction, a 180° turn away from sin and idols in the heart and toward God. When one repents, it is not a simple penance for guilt or a quick prayer for forgiveness, true repentance causes a change of heart and complete brokenness at one's detestable sin.

True About Face repentance brings change in the way we think. (Matthew 21:29.) God wants to influence and control our thinking. (2 Corinthians 10: 5, Philippians 4: 8.) When repentance comes and we change our way of thinking, it results in a distinct, observable, and definitional change in behavior.

When we hear and obey God when He issues an About Face, we can start in a new direction, free from the condemnation of sin and with new joy from a pure conscience before God. To continue in a new direction positioned for God's best, requires staying the course, marching ahead with resolve to do things God's way, not our way.

Second Peter 3:9 reminds us that all thanks belongs to God, as He is long suffering, not willing that any should perish, but that all should come to repentance. It's God will for all to come to repentance, doing an About Face as we turn to Him. He doesn't want one person to miss the opportunity for the gift He is offering! The ability to repent is in itself a gift from God, a direct result of God's goodness working in our lives (Romans 2:4). His *goodness* leads us toward repentance. He will lead us to repentance, but it is up to us to do an About Face.

As you continue your journey in Christ, humble yourself before the Commander in Chief and follow as He issues cadence. When He reveals areas of your life that need change, saying, "About Face!" respond to His orders and stay in step with Him as He leads. As our key verse says, if you humble yourself and turn from your sin, He will hear from heaven, will forgive your sin and heal your land.

If your About Face is a bit awkward or you wind up facing the wrong direction, not to worry! God will meet you right where you're at and will help you turn in the right direction. Forward, march!

FOR REFLECTION

1. In what areas of my life has God been bringing conviction of sin?

2. How have I responded to the conviction of the Holy Spirit? Have I listened and followed God's direction or have I ignored it?

3. God's goodness leads to repentance. What does this statement mean to me?

4. Reflect on the items listed in #1 above. Am I ready to do an About Face to turn from my sin, and start in the right direction? What scriptures can I stand on and use to renew my mind as I start in a new direction?

Reflect on what I am saying, for the Lord will give you insight into all this.
(2 Timothy 2:7)

REPENTANCE

Amazing Lord of life, I cry out to You for mercy. My life has been plagued with unrighteous living, ungodly thoughts and selfish actions. I need a new direction that only You can provide. I've failed in so many ways, Father, and I ask Your forgiveness as I've fallen short in Your sight. I see my sin and I want to do an About Face. I turn from my sin and turn toward You, God. Cleanse me of my wickedness and put me on Your path of righteousness.

OTHER AREAS OF REPENTANCE

Repent, then, and turn to God, so that your sins may be wiped out,
that times of refreshing may come from the Lord.
(Acts 3:19)

SUBMISSION

My God, my God! I have enlisted in Your Army and submit myself to Your authority. I will listen and respond to Your call, and will follow the path You have set before me. May sin be far from me as You cloak me in Your righteousness. I want Your will to be done in my life, O Most High God. I welcome Your help daily as I turn from the temptation of sin and fall into Your loving arms that will embrace me always. In Jesus' Name.

OTHER AREAS OF SUBMISSION

_____

_____

_____

Submit yourselves, then, to God.
(James 4:7)

FROM THE FATHER'S HEART

I am here always for you, My beloved one. I remove your sin stained clothes and clothe you in My glory and My righteousness. As I put my finger on areas of sinfulness, respond to My leading. Leave sin behind, turn from it quickly, and you will see My glory shine. The temptation of the evil one appears to entice you into sin, but it leads to death. My path of righteousness leads to life everlasting. Come. Follow Me to life everlasting.

PERSONAL WORD FROM MY FATHER

_____

_____

_____

Speak, LORD, for your servant is listening.
(1 Samuel 3:9)

DAY 16

MEDITATION

Compassion is part of God's nature and therefore, is part of my nature. Though I am moved with compassion toward others, I must stay in tune to the leading of the Holy Spirit in order to respond in line with God's plan. If He leads me to step in to help, I must obey. And if He leads me to step back, I must step back. If I step in when I'm supposed to step back, I can interfere with what God is doing in another's life. God sees the big picture; I only see a tiny piece of the picture.

May my meditation be pleasing to him, as I rejoice in the LORD.
(Psalm 104:34)

SCRIPTURE FOCUS

The LORD is good and does what is right;
he shows the proper path to those who go astray.
(Psalm 25:8, NLT)

What is my Father speaking to me through this Scripture?

DEVOTION FOR THE DAY

I liked the butcher and looked forward to visiting with him on shopping days. Sonny was easy to like. His countenance shined even brighter than his bleached cap, and his pearly white smile glistened next to his dark skin. Sonny's words uplifted his customers, putting an extra bounce in their step. "I can tell that you love the Lord, Sonny," I told him one day as he was preparing my meat order.

"Yes, I do!" he said, beaming. "How did you know?"

"Because I can see the joy of the Lord in you. That's why!" I told him.

One day, after exchanging our usual greetings and discussing the buys of the week, he said, "My electricity is going to be turned off tomorrow."

Although I didn't want to pry, I wanted to know the details, curious why he was about to lose his utilities. "Why?" I asked.

Sonny explained in detail, a long string of complicated events that had taken place in his life. He had lost his wife suddenly from a brain aneurism, was now living with a girlfriend, and an unplanned pregnancy had resulted in his new baby girl.

Suffering the consequences of choices he had made, he had fallen behind on his bills. He had received warnings from the electric company, he told me, but the cut-off date was tomorrow.

After we wrapped up our conversation, I wheeled my cart to the next grocery aisle. But my mind stayed on Sonny. Perusing my grocery list, thoughts swirled through my head. Compassion for his situation gripped me and I wanted to help.

Lord, I prayed silently, *should I give Sonny some money?* I wheeled into the next aisle, shuffling through my cereal coupons. Considering what I ought to do, I felt confident that my husband trusted me and would support me helping someone if I felt God was leading me.

Waiting in expectation for the Lord's answer, I fully anticipated a green light from God, along with a specific amount I was to give.

"No!" boomed in my heart.

No? I questioned. My face flushed, embarrassed at the thought of being too selfish to help someone, especially a fellow Christian! A battle raged inside. It didn't make sense to me that God would direct me not to give to someone in need. I shivered, picturing the newborn baby turning blue in a cold apartment.

Suspecting that I was failing to hear the voice of the Good Shepherd, I prepared to go ahead and give anyway. Turning my cart around, I headed toward the meat department.

"No!" I heard again. God had spoken, this time with undeniable authority.

"Back so soon?" Sonny asked when I rounded the corner.

"I just wanted to tell you one last thing," I said, the words escaping my lips without forethought, as if God had taken control of my mouth. "God is faithful, Sonny. If you do your part, He will do His part."

He smiled, absorbing the simple, yet profound words.

I didn't give Sonny money that day, and never knew what happened to him, or to his electricity as I never saw him again. But I did know that God was working in his life and that He would, indeed, be faithful. God, the only One who knows the details of Sonny's life, would continue to lead him and guide him.

Compassion, one of the beautiful traits of Jesus, moves us to love and help others in need. Sometimes, however, compassion can be misinterpreted as direction from the Holy Spirit.

Although needs are great around us, God does not always want us to step in to rescue His children. In fact, if we insert ourselves into people's lives at the wrong time or in the wrong manner, we can interfere with God's work. While He is trying to bring them to a new path, our misguided actions can instead further enable them to continue on the wrong path!

Be led by the Holy Spirit, listening carefully to and following the way in which He leads. Be willing to move forward when He says, "Go" and prepared to step back when He says, "No." And pray that others will be in tune to the Spirit of God too, that God might have His way in You, too.

FOR REFLECTION

1. Think back to a time I was moved with compassion toward someone in need. Recount the story.

2. Did I feel led to take action on this person's behalf? What did I do? As I examine my motives, what motivated me to help him or her?

3. What was the result of my actions? What did I learn from this situation?

4. Ask God to teach me about the subject of compassion as I search the gospels for times when Jesus was moved with compassion. What did I learn from Jesus?

Reflect on what I am saying, for the Lord will give you insight into all this.
(2 Timothy 2:7)

REPENTANCE

Holy Lord, forgive me for thinking I knew best how to help others in need. Forgive me for the times I've stepped into other people's lives when I should have stepped back. Forgive me for the times I haven't asked You for direction, then jumped in prematurely to rescue those I thought were drowning in life's circumstances. As I look back, I see that I may have interfered with Your plan by trying to rescue others from suffering. I'm sorry, O God, for trying to be a savior to others instead of pointing them to You, the one and only Savior of the world.

OTHER AREAS OF REPENTANCE

_____

_____

Repent, then, and turn to God, so that your sins may be wiped out,
that times of refreshing may come from the Lord.
(Acts 3:19)

SUBMISSION

Father of compassion, God of all comfort, here I am, Lord. I am available to You today. Use me as a tool to demonstrate Your compassion to others. Keep me, O Lord, from deception and protect me from those who might want to misuse or take advantage of my compassion. Please open my spiritual eyes and ears to see and hear the leading of Your Spirit. Activate the spirit of discernment so I will know when to step in to help and when to step back. Help me grow in compassion, while always pointing others to You, the one true God. In Jesus' Name.

OTHER AREAS OF SUBMISSION

_____

_____

Submit yourselves, then, to God.
(James 4:7)

FROM THE FATHER'S HEART

My little lamb, follow Me. Listen to My voice. You know My voice and can hear My voice through the many avenues through which I speak. You don't need to understand everything, nor do you need to figure out the details of My instruction. Just listen and obey as I show you the way. I am the Good Shepherd and will always lead you according to My will. My will is built on love and is flawless in every way.

PERSONAL WORD FROM MY FATHER

Speak, LORD, for your servant is listening.
(I Samuel 3:9)

DAY 17

MEDITATION

I am in the world, but not of this world. While on this earth, I have the privilege of choosing what I see, hear and speak. The input I allow through these avenues will impact the output that comes through my life. That with which I fill my heart will be evidenced in what comes from my mouth. I am a living epistle for all people to read.

May my meditation be pleasing to him,
as I rejoice in the LORD.
(Psalm 104:34)

SCRIPTURE FOCUS

For it is written: "Be holy, because I am holy."
(1 Peter 1:16)

What is my Father speaking to me through this Scripture?

DEVOTION FOR THE DAY

I woke up one morning with a strong sense that God wanted to impart a special message to me before I launched into my day. "Speak, Lord, Your servant is listening," I prayed.

"Keep a strap on your yap!" He seemed to whisper in my heart. That wasn't exactly what I had in mind for a special word from the Lord!

After setting my pride aside, I examined my heart to see why God would find it necessary to breathe those jolting, yet loving words into my spirit.

I did need a yap strap. I *had* been quick to respond to others when asked for counsel—instead of taking time to ponder and pray about the answer first. I *had* blurted out feelings and opinions prematurely—instead of waiting for God's perfect timing. I *had* allowed careless words to flow like a river—when they should have been prayerfully taken to God for wisdom first. And I *had* repeated other's misguided words—instead of burying them in the sea of forgetfulness.

Reflecting on the occasions I had neglected to guard my mouth, I quickly ran out of fingers on which to count! Only the night before, I had offered a responsorial opinion when my opinion had not been solicited. Only a day earlier, I had spoken out of turn, missing an opportunity to minister grace to one experiencing a trial-laden day. And the previous week, I had offered advice based on emotion and past experience instead of seeking and sharing God's perspective.

The Bible says, "Be quick to listen, slow to speak, slow to anger" (James 1:19, NRSV). Yet many, like me, often reverse the order, acting on the carnal interpretation of James 1:19: "Be quick to speak and slow to listen." Following God's direction—being quick to listen and slow to speak—brings a harvest of the fruit of the Spirit, but reversing the order—being quick to speak and slow to listen—breeds rotten fruit—and a foot in the mouth!

If we listen first—to what others say and to what God says—heavenly anointed words can flow at the right time. And more often than not, speaking with God's perspective and in His timing requires fewer words. Proverbs 10:19 offers a word of wisdom to those with unrestrained yap issues: "When words are many, transgression is not lacking, but the prudent are restrained in speech" (NRSV).

For help in getting a strap for our yap, we can call out to the One who can help, and pray, "Set a guard over my mouth, O LORD; keep watch over the door of my lips" (Psalm 141:3, NRSV).

To effectively guard our mouth, we must also guard our heart. The Bible says, "Out of the abundance of the heart the mouth speaks" (Matthew 12:34, NRSV). If we store good things in our heart, good will come from our mouth; and if we store evil in our heart, evil will flow from our mouth. The mouth eventually catches up with the heart.

You—and others—will know the contents of your heart by listening to what comes from your mouth. What a sobering thought!

Two key senses—hearing and sight—affect the contents of our heart. If our eyes and ears receive the right heart input, we'll find greater success in bringing the right heart output from our mouth.

Mark 4:24 says, "Take heed what you hear" (NKJV). Listening to and partaking in conversations that honor God and build others fills our heart with good. But participating in dialogue dripping with gossip and foolish talk fills our heart with evil.

I remember hearing a false report about an honorable man of God. "Nonsense!" I said, and discarded the slanderous report. Some, instead of squelching the lie and believing the best of God's servant, played right into the enemy's hands, listening to and entertaining the wrong report.

Matthew 6:22-23 says, "The eye is the lamp of the body. If your eyes are good, your whole body will be full of light. But if your eyes are bad, your whole body will be full of darkness."

The media abounds with ungodly material, creating endless opportunities to paint evil imaginations in our mind. Looking at inappropriate material—intentionally or unintentionally—leaves an imprint on our memory, which can be challenging to erase. If not eradicated, those images can lead to wrong thoughts and eventually sinful actions.

With masses of ungodly material clamoring for our attention, we must purpose to guard our eyes and ears, even if it means turning off the television or signing off the Internet! Without an alert guard at the doorpost of our heart and home, our heart can fill with evil and our conscience can become seared without us realizing it.

What we listen to and look at today affects what we think about tomorrow. If we fill our heart with good, guarding our ears and eyes, the words of our mouth and the meditation of our heart will be pleasing in God's sight.

After acknowledging and repenting for my yap problem, I lingered in God's presence a bit longer, receiving His correction, and His unconditional love. With yap strap in place, I leapt out of bed, spiritually energized and determined to hear no evil, see no evil and speak no evil.

FOR REFLECTION

I. With a humble heart, examine my mouth. Have the words of my mouth built others up and honored God or have they been destructive and dishonorable?

2. With a humble heart, examine what I've allowed myself to watch or see. Have I guarded what I allow my eyes to gaze upon or has my conscience been seared?

3. With a humble heart, examine what I've allowed myself to hear. Do I listen to inappropriate talk, gossip and slander? What standards have I set for movies and television? Have I loosened my standards?

4. In view of the preceding questions, what steps can I take to hear no evil, speak no evil and see no evil?

Reflect on what I am saying, for the Lord will give you insight into all this.
(2 Timothy 2:7)

REPENTANCE

Lord God, as I examine my heart, I come before You with a humbled heart of repentance. I have spoken, listened to and looked at things of this world that are dishonorable to You and that grieve Your Spirit. Cleanse me of my sin, Father, through the shed blood of Jesus. Forgive me, dear God, for knowingly and unknowingly entertaining sin through the world's means of entertainment. Help me, Lord Jesus, to guard my heart, my eyes, my ears and my mouth. Strengthen me and give me wisdom to lift up a standard in me that will represent You honorably.

OTHER AREAS OF REPENTANCE

_____

_____

_____

Repent, then, and turn to God, so that your sins may be wiped out,
that times of refreshing may come from the Lord.
(Acts 3:19)

SUBMISSION

Take my mouth, Lord, and help me speak words that align with Your Word to build and encourage others. Take my ears, Lord, and help me listen to words that bring life. Take my eyes, Lord, and help me look upon what is pure and lovely. Put guards around my mouth, my ears and my eyes, that I might honor You. In Jesus' Name.

OTHER AREAS OF SUBMISSION

Submit yourselves, then, to God.
(James 4:7)

FROM THE FATHER'S HEART

I have put you in this world, but you are not of this world. I have chosen you as My representative on the earth. Though much evil surrounds you, I shall enable and strengthen you to remain pure in My sight. But you must have My ways foremost in your heart and resist the ways of the world. You must have My Word written on the tablet of your heart and you must walk close with Me. Together, we will radiate My glory for all to see.

PERSONAL WORD FROM MY FATHER

Speak, LORD, for your servant is listening.
(1 Samuel 3:9)

DAY 18

MEDITATION

God has a perfect plan for my life and has provided everything I need to accomplish that plan. If I seek and follow my loving Father's plan, I will find peace as I walk out His divinely orchestrated plan. If my priorities are His priorities, I will find perfect peace, plentiful provision and sufficient strength. If I lack peace, provision and strength, He will show me areas needing adjustment, if I am willing to listen and obey.

May my meditation be pleasing to him, as I rejoice in the LORD.
(Psalm 104:34)

SCRIPTURE FOCUS

I know, O LORD, that a man's life is not his own;
it is not for man to direct his steps.
(Jeremiah 10:23)

What is my Father speaking to me through this Scripture?

_____

_____

_____

DEVOTION FOR THE DAY

Walk. Eat. These two words, known and understood by Cooper, our old yellow Lab, were top dog priorities.

Hearing W-A-L-K, Cooper leapt from a sound sleep, bounded for the door and barked while dancing in circles. If someone slipped on shoes or grabbed the leash, his dance rendition started again. Seeing a hefty hound lift all four feet at once is quite a sight!

E-A-T provoked a similar response. When our daughter Emily stirred in the morning, Cooper dashed into her room, began his leap and spin jig, then stuck to Emily like glue until she headed for his food bin.

Cooper once faced a doggy dilemma when my husband ventured out to scoop Cooper's breakfast. After dishing up the canine nuggets, Tom grabbed his shoes and the leash, then set the food dish in its normal spot.

Cooper panicked as his priorities teased him. His mouth watered at the silver bowlful of luscious morsels. Yet his master stood, leash in hand, ready for a walk.

Cooper danced. He eyed Tom, then the food, then the leash. Walk. Eat. Walk. Eat. Running back and forth from Tom to the food, Cooper couldn't decide what to do. Unable to prioritize his priorities, he ran in circles, confused.

After gobbling a crunchy mouthful, Cooper changed his mind and dashed for the door. His tail swept the floor while he waited for Tom's signal. Leashed and ready to run, Cooper leapt out the door and danced down the sidewalk, dragging Tom behind.

After a brisk morning stroll, the happy hound bolted through the door, sped to his food, and wolfed down his breakfast. Nourished and exercised, he slept through the rest of the morning.

Does God witness a similar scenario in us? Are we running in circles because our priorities are out of order?

God took the guesswork out of the priority puzzle. Although everyone has personal priorities, first things first. *God wants to be first in all things*

(Exodus 20:3). Although people, ministry, career, hobbies and money compete for position, *nothing* can come before God. Give Him, and His unchanging Word, first place. Everything else follows.

Without God's blessing on our activities, we can strive and sweat, yet produce little fruit. Proverbs 16:9 says, "In his heart a man plans his course, but the LORD determines his steps." God determines our steps day by day and helps us prioritize moment by moment. If we make God's priorities our priorities, everything falls into place and all will be well.

In the midst of publishing my first book, co-authoring a second book, freelance writing, and attending Bible College, not to mention being a wife and mother, the Lord prompted me to write another book. Although I'd prayed about this project for more than a year, the Lord stunned me with His go-ahead at such an inconvenient time.

"Now, Lord?" I questioned. "But, but, but... I have so many *other* priorities right now!" Yet, sensing I'd received marching orders from God, I began the project.

The tasks at hand seemed impossible, yet fueled with God's strength, purpose and direction, I was fully persuaded that all could be accomplished. "I can do all things through Christ who strengthens me" (Philippians 4:13, NKJV), became my constant companion.

A constant flurry of demanding pursuits continued for two years. Yet, because God had ordained the activities and provided me with blue prints and strength through prayer, every project was fruitful and my marriage and family flourished in the process.

Years earlier, while juggling an overflowing plate of responsibilities, I fretted regularly. If nobody stepped up to the plate when needs arose, I stepped in without consulting God. While I rescued every needy project, my marriage and family rattled out of balance. Physical and spiritual exhaustion plagued me. After complete burnout, I wept at Jesus' feet, surrendering my empty self and overloaded schedule to God.

God opened my eyes to my flawed, unbalanced life. After I repented, God helped me discover His divinely orchestrated plan for my life. When opportunities arose, I sought His will and didn't move until He gave the go ahead.

Good activities aren't necessarily God activities. If we exhaust our time on activities God never intended for us to do, we risk missing out on God-ordained activities, and can fall short of accomplishing His divine purpose. If we overload ourselves, we can spin our wheels toiling on unfruitful projects while getting nowhere.

In Old Testament times, the priests wore linen garments when entering the temple gates of the inner courts to minister to the Lord. Garments made of wool or any other material that might cause one to perspire in God's presence were forbidden (Ezekiel 44:18).

The first time sweat is mentioned in the Bible is after Adam and Eve sinned in the Garden of Eden. "Cursed is the ground because of you, through painful toil you will eat of it all the days of your life...By the sweat of your brow you will eat your food" (Genesis 3:17-19).

When the ground was cursed, it couldn't yield fruit without human effort. Fleshly effort produces sweat. Without God's blessing on our activities, we strive and sweat, yet produce little fruit.

Are you sweating and toiling to make things work? Are you doing what God called you to do? Did your activity spring forth from prayer in God's presence?. God ordained activities don't require you to sweat it out. Spiritual work is God's work, and when He works, you don't need to expend unnecessary effort. If you're sweating it out, you may be serving your own agenda instead of God's agenda. If you're fueled with God's ability to accomplish all He called you to do, striving and toiling are unnecessary.

What's on your agenda today? Let God set your course, then don't sweat it!

FOR REFLECTION

1. What are my top five priorities? List them. How much of my available time is assigned to each priority listed? How do I feel about where I'm spending the majority of my time?

2. Did I create my priority list or did man create it for me? Was God involved in establishing my activities? Explain.

3. Where does God fit in my priority list? Have I made time for prayer and study of His Word? Have I given myself permission to allow times of rest when I have no obligations, no distractions and no work? If not, do I need to schedule some downtime?

4. What priorities are causing me personal conflict? What priorities are causing conflict within my family? Pay particular attention to those activities that cause me to strive and sweat to get the job done. Talk to God about the conflicts, ask Him if I need to re-prioritize and document what He shows me.

Reflect on what I am saying, for the Lord will give you insight into all this.
(2 Timothy 2:7)

REPENTANCE

Lord Jesus, I have been running in circles, striving and sweating to accomplish many things that may not have been ordained by You. I'm out of control. Father, I don't want to invest any more precious time in something that will burn up as wood, hay or stubble. Although I have claimed that You were my top priority, my actions have indicated otherwise. Dear God, forgive me. I'm sorry, Father, for taking our relationship for granted. Forgive me for striving and sweating to get jobs done when I'm not sure you've assigned the jobs to me in the first place. Have mercy on me, God, a sinner.

OTHER AREAS OF REPENTANCE

Repent, then, and turn to God, so that your sins may be wiped out, that times of refreshing may come from the Lord.
(Acts 3:19)

SUBMISSION

Most High God, precious Savior, I offer You my life today. I offer You my flawed priority list and ask You to transform my priority list into Your priority list. I want only what You want. Take away any wood, hay or stubble and replace it with purpose filled action. Father, align my will with Your will. Align my schedule with Your schedule. I don't want to run in circles any longer, Father. May Your peace, Your provision and Your strength lead me on a steady course as You guide me on Your perfectly paved path of purpose. In Jesus' Name.

OTHER AREAS OF SUBMISSION

Submit yourselves, then, to God.
(James 4:7)

FROM THE FATHER'S HEART

Do you know, Child, that I delight in you? Do you know how proud I am of you? I smile on you today, and welcome you as you come to Me for guidance. I've watched you run in circles trying to please Me. But you need not run, you need not strive. My plan is a perfect plan of peace and as you set your course to honor Me and My plan, My perfect peace will always go before you. When you don't sense My peace, stop. If My peace is not present, I say, "Do not move." Follow My peace and you will find great joy in serving Me. My peace I give you today, My beloved.

PERSONAL WORD FROM MY FATHER

Speak, LORD, for your servant is listening.
(1 Samuel 3:9)

DAY 19

MEDITATION

Because God is a just God, a price had to be paid for the punishment of my sin. Although I deserved eternal separation from God, sickness and disease, my Father loved me so much that He sent Jesus, His only begotten Son to pay the penalty for my sin. The Lamb of God offers a love-laced package deal, given freely to all who will receive. Every drop of shed blood said, "You are forgiven." Every stripe on His back said, "You are healed." I receive. In Jesus' Name, I receive.

May my meditation be pleasing to him, as I rejoice in the LORD.
(Psalm 104:34)

SCRIPTURE FOCUS

Christ redeemed us from the curse of the law by becoming a curse for us,
for it is written: "Cursed is everyone who is hung on a tree."
(Galatians 3:13)

What is my Father speaking to me through this Scripture?

DAY 19

DEVOTION FOR THE DAY

My brother Jim and I love package deals. We often tease one another about our built-in radar for bargains and claim to have been raised on "Frugal Loops". We're always on the lookout for coupons, buy-one-get-one-free programs and best of all, package deals.

God offers the world's best package deal ever. A paralyzed man was a recipient of this package long ago when Jesus walked the earth.

Traveling around the region of Galilee, Jesus had been preaching, driving out demons and healing. When He returned to Capernaum, news had spread about Him and crowds gathered.

Four men arrived at the house where Jesus was staying, carrying a paralyzed man on a mat. Because the place was packed full of visitors, they realized they couldn't get their paralyzed friend through the crowd. Cutting a hole through the roof, they lowered him down in front of Jesus. Seeing their faith in action, Jesus introduced part of His package deal, saying, "My child, your sins are forgiven."

The teachers of religious law, knowing that only God could forgive sins, considered Jesus' statement blasphemy. But they didn't understand His package deal! Luke 5:23 NLT tells us that Jesus then said, "'Is it easier to say [to the paralyzed man], "Your sins are forgiven," or "Stand up and walk"? So I will prove to you that the Son of Man has the authority on earth to forgive sins.' Then Jesus turned to the paralyzed man and said, 'Stand up, pick up your mat, and go home!'"

Happy to receive the package deal, the man jumped up, grabbed his mat, and walked out through the stunned onlookers. They were all amazed and praised God, exclaiming, "We've never seen anything like this before!"

What if we had witnessed this remarkable scene? Would we be stunned by Jesus' actions, shocked at the miracle that unfolded before our eyes? Would we realize the best package deal since the beginning of time?

Sin and sickness came into the world as Satan's package deal, creating a great need for God's package deal. Deuteronomy 28 lists the many curses of the Law that would come if God's people disobeyed Him. Although many sicknesses and diseases are mentioned in the curse, God added, "Also every sickness, and every plague, which is not written in the book of this law, them will the LORD bring upon thee, until thou be destroyed" (Deuteronomy 28:61, KJV). *Every* sickness and disease is part of the curse, without exception.

Those who depend on the Law to make them right with God are under His curse, for the Scriptures say, "All who rely on observing the law are under a curse, for it is written: 'Cursed is everyone who does not continue to do everything written in the Book of the Law'" (Galatians 3:10).

No human being could possibly live up to the Law, even if they tried. Not even one, as *all* have sinned (Romans 3:23). God is a God of justice and therefore, a price had to be paid for sin. But because God so loved the world, He made a way through Jesus. Galatians 3:13 says, "Christ redeemed us from the curse of the law by becoming a curse for us, for it is written: 'Cursed is everyone who is hung on a tree.'"

We've been redeemed by the blood of the Lamb! We have been freed from sin and sickness and disease! Jesus took the punishment for our sin, redeeming us from the curse. Instead of us suffering eternal death and destruction, He paid the price so we wouldn't have to. "For God made Christ, who never sinned, to be the offering for our sin, so that we could be made right with God through Christ" (2 Corinthians 5:21, NLT).

Jesus Christ, shedding His blood, suffering, dying and rising from dead, freed us from the penalty of sin *and* freed us from sickness and disease, the penalty of the Law. It's a package deal!

Jesus could have told the paralytic either, "Your sins are forgiven" or "pick up your mat and go home," as they were both part of the same package. Forgiveness comes with healing and healing comes with forgiveness. God's package deal belongs to you.

Have I got a deal for you! His Name is Jesus!

FOR REFLECTION

I. What has been my belief about God's ability to heal physical sickness and disease? On what have those beliefs been based?

2. Is Jesus Christ my Lord and Savior? Explain the difference between "Lord" and "Savior."

3. What package deal did Jesus offer the paralyzed man in Luke 5? Jesus told the paralytic that he was forgiven, then told him he could pick up his mat and go home. What is the relation between these two statements?

4. Read Deuteronomy 28, then read Galatians 3:10-13. Are there any sicknesses or diseases not covered in the curse of the Law in Deuteronomy 28? What does, "Christ redeemed us from the curse of the law by becoming a curse for us" mean to me?

Reflect on what I am saying, for the Lord will give you insight into all this.
(2 Timothy 2:7)

REPENTANCE

Lord God, I kneel before You and plead for mercy and grace. It is only by Your grace that I have not perished for my lack of knowledge. Jesus, Your demonstration of love awes me and paves the way for my forgiveness. I repent of my unbelief, Father. I repent of my lack of knowledge of Your Word. I didn't realize the great price that was paid so that I could not only be forgiven of sin, but that I might walk in complete wholeness and health. I'm sorry, Father, for willingly accepting flawed teachings without digging into Your Word for the truth. Today, I accept Jesus as my Savior, and as my Healer.

OTHER AREAS OF REPENTANCE

_____

_____

_____

Repent, then, and turn to God, so that your sins may be wiped out,
that times of refreshing may come from the Lord.
(Acts 3:19)

SUBMISSION

Jesus, Your Word says that You sent Your Word and healed us. I receive that living Word today. I receive You as Healer. Write Your truths on the tablet of my heart that it might illuminate my path and light the way for others. Expand my understanding of Your Word where healing is concerned. Use my hands to lay hands on the sick. Release Your healing anointing in me and make me a demonstration of Your healing power. Thank You, Father, that by the stripes of Your Son Jesus, I am healed. In Jesus' Name.

OTHER AREAS OF SUBMISSION

_____

_____

_____

Submit yourselves, then, to God.
(James 4:7)

FROM THE FATHER'S HEART

I AM the Great Physician. I AM your Lord. I AM your Savior. I AM your Healer. I have made provision for everything you need, body, soul and spirit. As you grow in knowledge of Me and My Word, you will walk in a greater understanding and a greater demonstration of My power. My people perish for their lack of understanding. My people perish, for they don't know Me. But you shall know Me. When you seek Me, you will find Me, when you seek Me with all of your heart.

PERSONAL WORD FROM MY FATHER

Speak, LORD, for your servant is listening.
(1 Samuel 3:9)

DAY 20

MEDITATION

God guards my path and protects my way. He laid out the entire plan for my life before even one day came to pass. He knows my past, He knows my today and He knows my future. I can trust Him with my life, knowing that He has a good plan He designed for my good and for His glory. If I trust Him with all my heart and do not lean on my own understanding, He will guard my heart and my mind in Christ Jesus.

May my meditation be pleasing to him, as I rejoice in the LORD.
(Psalm 104:34)

SCRIPTURE FOCUS

So let's not get tired of doing what is good.
At just the right time we will reap a harvest of blessing if we don't give up.
(Galatians 6:9, NLT)

What is my Father speaking to me through this Scripture?

DEVOTION FOR THE DAY

Our first baby was on the way! What wondrous news, learning I was pregnant for the first time. Although it would be several months before visible signs would evidence the pregnancy, life grew within, hidden away until the appointed time of arrival. Nine months of critical stages of development progressed as the baby matured and prepared for survival outside the womb.

While my son's frame was being formed within, I waited. And waited. Waiting patiently isn't my strongest virtue, especially when waiting includes morning sickness, swollen ankles, weight gain, indigestion, and back pain! My increasing discomfort caused me to wish that our son would arrive ahead of schedule. Yet God, whose timing is perfect for everything, had established an appointed time for James' arrival on the earth. *The right time.*

God has an appointed time for you to birth that which He is creating within you. The promises and dreams you carry in your spiritual womb, however, must reach full term and be birthed at *the right time*: God's appointed time.

Jesus came to earth as Son of God and Son of man, arriving right on time, at God's appointed, or *kairos* time.* Galatians 4:4-5 NLT says, "When the right time came, God sent his Son, born of a woman, subject to the law. God sent him to buy freedom for us who were slaves to the law, so that he could adopt us as his very own children." He was not ahead of God's schedule or behind God's schedule. He came *at the right time.*

A *kairos* time is an exact moment that shall come to pass at the precise moment in God's timetable. It's an opportune time, not just a succession of moments. A *kairos* time is a critical or desired point in time, a moment of great importance and significance when something is ready, it's a period marked by distinct conditions. It's *the right time.*

---

* *Hebrew-Greek Key Word Study Bible*, "kairos" (Goodrick-Kohlenberger #2789), p. 1635-36

From the day of Jesus' birth to the day of His hour of suffering, death and resurrection, everything took place according to God's perfect plan. Jesus understood and accepted His Father's timetable, knowing that God's plan was a flawless one.

Jesus also knew when it wasn't the right time. While teaching in the temple, Jesus often upset the religious people. Although they wanted to seize and kill Him, they couldn't lay a hand on Him, the Bible says, because *His time had not yet come* (John 7:30). When He caused a stir in the temple, Jesus was not arrested because *His time had not yet come* (John 8:20). When His brothers encouraged Him to go to the Jewish Festival of Shelters to display His miracle working power, Jesus said it *wasn't the right time* for Him to go (John 7:7). And at the wedding at Cana in Galilee, Jesus told his mother that *His time had not yet come* when she told Him they were out of wine (John 2:4).

But when *the right time* neared, Jesus knew it. Telling his disciples to make preparations for the Passover, He said *His appointed time was near* (Matthew 26:18). Before the Passover feast, Jesus knew that *the time had come* for Him to leave this world and go to His Father (John 13:1).

Jesus, submitted to His Father's divine timetable to fulfill His divine purpose, arrived on the earth and left the earth at just *the right time*. To fulfill our divine purpose, we must submit to our Father's divine timetable as well, willing to wait for *the right time*.

We sometimes think it's the right time, then discover it's the wrong time. Our youngest son, Joe, was scheduled to arrive on February 14. But on February 12, I went into labor so we headed to the hospital. Once we arrived, however, labor stopped. Although I walked around the hospital trying to help the labor progress, it had come to a standstill. They sent me back home to wait, as it wasn't the right time for Joe's arrival. Then, on February 14, a glorious Valentine's Day in 1994, Joseph arrived. Right on time!

Human nature wants to speed up the passage of time so we can birth God's plan when *we* think we're ready, but God has a *right* time. If we follow His timetable, we won't give birth prematurely and we won't be over due. We'll be *right on time*.

FOR REFLECTION

1. What do I believe is the ideal way to discern the "right" time and the "wrong" time? How can I identify each?

2. Give an example of a time in which I acted at the "right" time and an example of a time in which I acted at the "wrong" time. What were the results of both situations?

3. Has frustration or weariness ever caused me to push a door open before God's ideal time? What happened? What did I learn from the experience?

4. Am I tired of waiting for something specific to come to pass? Explain. Do I need to release this situation to God and surrender my plan to His plan?

Reflect on what I am saying, for the Lord will give you insight into all this.
(2 Timothy 2:7)

REPENTANCE

Lord God, I am guilty of demanding my own way once again, instead of trusting You to bring the details of my life together in Your timing. I've failed to trust You countless times and often forget that Your plan is a perfect plan that You brought to life through Your unfailing love for me. Please forgive me, Father, and teach me to learn from the error of my ways.

OTHER AREAS OF REPENTANCE

Repent, then, and turn to God, so that your sins may be wiped out,
that times of refreshing may come from the Lord.
(Acts 3:19)

SUBMISSION

God, I bring my expectations and dreams to Your altar and offer them as a sacrifice unto You. I don't want anything You have planned for my life to come to pass before its time. I don't want to birth anything prematurely, yet I don't want to be overdue. I want to be right on time according to Your will. I surrender, Lord, all that I am and all that I want to do, to You. I surrender my family and my loved ones to You. I surrender my work, my ministry and my goals to You. I surrender all. Have Your way in me. In Jesus' Name.

OTHER AREAS OF SUBMISSION

Submit yourselves, then, to God.
(James 4:7)

FROM THE FATHER'S HEART

I understand your frustration and I understand your weariness as you wait for My perfect plan to come to pass. My plan is a perfect one, and it will come to pass just as I planned. I know the beginning from the end. I am already in your tomorrow, with a wondrous plan for you. If only you knew what I have in store for you! It will be well worth the wait, my little one. If you trust Me and rest in Me, you will see that all will be well!

PERSONAL WORD FROM MY FATHER

Speak, LORD, for your servant is listening.
(1 Samuel 3:9)

DAY 21

MEDITATION

My ways are not God's ways and my thoughts are not His thoughts. Though much has happened that I do not understand, and many questions remain unanswered, I can choose to trust my heavenly Father, who loves me. My God is a God of love. He *IS* love, and always acts in love. Though I don't always understand the details of my circumstances, I choose to trust in the Lord with all of my heart.

May my meditation be pleasing to him, as I rejoice in the LORD.
(Psalm 104:34)

SCRIPTURE FOCUS

"For my thoughts are not your thoughts,
neither are your ways my ways," declares the LORD.
(Isaiah 55:8)

What is my Father speaking to me through this Scripture?

_____

_____

_____

DEVOTION FOR THE DAY

"Why?" I suspect that God hears that question more than any other. I've certainly asked that question more than my share of times, especially when nothing makes sense. Paty's death was one of those times.

Paty intrigued me from the start. At first, her hesitancy to delve beyond casual small talk seemed apparent, yet I sensed her unspoken desire for a willing friend to help her tear down the invisible fortress she had built around herself. "Lord," I petitioned, "help me be a friend."

In February of 1998, Paty's feet, toes and fingers began to swell. Achy joints stifled her diminishing energy. Suspicious of Paty's alarming symptoms, doctors ordered full body, head, bone and blood scans which revealed three tumors in the upper and lower right lung. Paty had cancer.

In surgery to remove her lung, the surgeon discovered the tumor encroached on her pulmonary artery; removal of the tumor would kill her. They closed her up, leaving the cancerous lung in tact.

I spent weary hours sitting at Paty's bedside following surgery. Only the eerie rhythm of bleeping monitors kept me company. Studying Paty as she lay in her bed, I wondered what her innermost thoughts were.

Doctors released Paty from the hospital and began aggressive chemotherapy and radiation treatment to shrink the tumor. I sent her many cards, starting each one, "Dear Precious Paty," as Paty had indeed become precious to me.

One treasured note I received back read, "When I asked God for a friend, He sent you." Paty's walls were tumbling down.

Additional radiation fought the relentless cancer. My now bald, swollen-faced friend became increasingly beautiful to me. In the midst of her suffering, Paty's staunchness had melted away while her inner beauty emerged.

After becoming disoriented and collapsing, Paty was hospitalized once again, beckoning her parents and children home from around the country. Paty's family, including her daughter and daughter-in-law who were both months away from giving birth, gathered at the hospital.

Paty's doctor entered her room while I was visiting, questioning Paty about her symptoms. Realizing the doctor was about to break critical news, I felt suffocated.

A body scan showed four new tumors spreading to her brain. Because the location of the brain tumors made surgical removal high risk, the family opted for radiation as a final attempt to shrink the spreading tumors.

Lightheaded, I realized I'd been holding my breath while the doctor spoke. I quickly left the hospital and headed home, weeping silently for Paty's continued trial ahead. I continued to pray for a miracle, yet wondered if Paty would live to see her two grandchildren born.

Our relationship grew, even through long periods of sitting together in silence. I trusted God to put His joy on my face during our visits, as I felt increasingly discouraged by Paty's failing condition. I sensed death standing at her door, yet I couldn't let go of the hope that God would work a miracle.

Standing at the foot of her bed one day, I jabbered about my day's happenings. Paty didn't respond. Stopping mid-sentence, I inched my way to Paty's side. Gripping her hand to my heart, I searched her face. Empty eyes stared back at me.

"Paty" I said, "do you know who I am?"

Paty studied me. Her bedside clock ticked as her questioning eyes sought my identity.

"...Mary?...Nancy?...ah..." Paty didn't know me. My precious Paty, as I had known, was gone.

Paty died on June 17, 1999, shortly after our last visit. Having held two new grandchildren in her frail arms, she left for her final destination after a long and hard fought battle with cancer.

"Why?" I cried out to God, desperate for understanding. Paty had prayed the right prayers, stood on the right healing scriptures, received the right ministry. She had done everything right. "Why, God? Why did she die?" I cried. But silence rang from the heavens.

Sitting in prayer early one morning, I closed my eyes as the sun streamed in. Overcome with sadness at the loss of my precious Paty, I petitioned God one last time, "Why?"

Healing tears rolled from my eyes as I realized I didn't need to understand the reason for Paty's death. God had answered my prayers, allowing me to help my friend break down the walls surrounding her. By loving my friend on her journey of trial, I had found the precious woman who lived inside the fortress walls that no longer surrounded her in eternity.

Paty wasn't the first friend I believed experienced a premature death. And she wasn't the last. It wasn't the last time, either, that I asked God, "Why?" When we face trials that don't make sense, we can choose to trust God in spite of our lack of understanding. God is sovereign. His ways are not our ways, and His thoughts are not our thoughts.

I like the way Beth Moore views trials like my friend Paty faced. Beth explains that sometimes God delivers us *from* the trial, sometimes He delivers us *through* the trial, and sometimes He takes us through the trial and into the arms of Jesus. If Paty were able, I'm confident that she would want us to know that she got the best option!

FOR REFLECTION

1. Have I ever lost a loved one whose death made no sense to me? Have I suffered another loss that I didn't understand? Explain.

2. How did I respond to the described situations? What was my response to God? What was my response to others? Did this situation drive me closer to God or further away from Him?

3. What questions did I want to ask God about this loss? In reviewing my list of questions, which questions has God answered? Which questions are still unanswered?

4. When I am ready, I can bring my unanswered questions to God. Am I willing to release my unresolved issue to God in spite of not having answers? I can tell my Father what I feel about my losses and then be still and listen for His voice. What is He speaking to me today?

Reflect on what I am saying, for the Lord will give you insight into all this.
(2 Timothy 2:7)

REPENTANCE

God of love, I see the error of my ways. I've often questioned You when I haven't understood the circumstances of life. I've blamed You for taking what is precious to me and I've accused You of not caring about me and my loved ones. Glorious Father, forgive me of my great sinfulness. You are faithful! Your ways are perfect. Create in me a new heart, O God, that trusts You completely in spite of what circumstances I may face.

O<small>THER AREAS OF REPENTANCE</small>

_____

_____

_____

Repent, then, and turn to God, so that your sins may be wiped out,
that times of refreshing may come from the Lord.
(Acts 3:19)

SUBMISSION

Father God, Lord of the universe, I've been troubled by unanswered questions. Today, I give You my questions. I will trust You in spite of unanswered questions. I've wavered in my faith because I haven't understood situations that You've allowed. Today, I give you my lack of understanding. I will trust You in spite of my lack of understanding. I put my trust in You, and will go forth with confidence knowing that every detail of my life is in Your faithful hands. In Jesus' Name.

O<small>THER AREAS OF SUBMISSION</small>

_____

_____

_____

Submit yourselves, then, to God.
(James 4:7)

FROM THE FATHER'S HEART

I surround you with My favor as with a shield, My precious one. You can walk daily with confidence in Me, knowing that all I allow is part of My divine plan. It pleases Me when you trust Me when nothing makes

sense. It delights Me when you rejoice in Me, even when your surroundings seem to contradict what you believe is right. I am good, always. I love you, always. And My plan is a perfect plan, always. As you trust Me with that which you do not understand, you will see My glorious plan unfold, all for your good and for My glory!

PERSONAL WORD FROM MY FATHER

_____

_____

_____

Speak, LORD, for your servant is listening.
(1 Samuel 3:9)

DAY 22

MEDITATION

As I live to please God, I can live in complete peace. I have no fear of man or what man can do to me. Man's opinion of me is irrelevant. I live for the pleasure of my loving Father, who watches over me every moment. My desire is to enter His glory to hear, "Well done, my good and faithful servant!" I will not forget who I am in Christ, I will not forget that I'm about my Father's business and I won't forget that I represent Christ in the earth. I may be the only Jesus some will ever see.

May my meditation be pleasing to him, as I rejoice in the LORD.
(Psalm 104:34)

SCRIPTURE FOCUS

Let love and faithfulness never leave you; bind them around your neck,
write them on the tablet of your heart. Then you will
win favor and a good name in the sight of God and man.
(Proverbs 3:3-4)

What is my Father speaking to me through this Scripture?

_____

_____

_____

DEVOTION FOR THE DAY

"Your kids are awesome," I told my dear friend, Lucy Laslo, one day over coffee.

"They really couldn't go wrong," she said, smiling. "I sent them off every day with God's blessing, and I always told them, 'Don't forget who you are, what you're about and Who you represent.'"

Lucy's words lodged in my spirit, provoking me to put her words of wisdom into action. From that day forward, I sent my kids to school with a blessing, reminding them, "Don't forget who you are, what you're about and Who you represent." Although it appeared at times that it went in one ear and out the other, I hoped the words would seep in and soak their spirits throughout the day, driving them to make the right choices. "The choices you make," I'd tell the kids, "are forming your reputation and affecting the way you represent Jesus to others."

In my early years, I made many wrong choices that created a reputation of which I was not proud. Yet when I met Jesus and began my journey in Him, I started learning who I was _in Him_ and what I was about _in Him_. I longed to represent Him in the earth honorably. Christ received me, as He does everyone, as I was, an imperfect human being. And today, still imperfect and capable of error and failures, He still receives me—and you!

God sees us much differently than we see ourselves. He sees us as we are in Christ. Looking through His scope, He sees the finished product. Our limited vision enables us to see only what is in front of us, and with the devil's help, our errors and failures are often magnified.

God cleanses us and moves us forward when we repent of our failures. Others however, don't always offer the same grace that God makes available. Our past reputation, like the Apostle Paul learned, can follow us, even when we're on the right track.

Mightily used of God, having written a good portion of the New Testament, Paul called himself the "chief of sinners." Before his conversion, when he was called Saul, Paul gave his stamp of approval as the Apostle Stephen was stoned to death. Prior to putting his faith in Jesus, he was known for persecution and abuse of Christians. Everything changed on the road to Damascus though, when God, pouring out His grace and mercy, grabbed hold of Paul's heart.

Although God radically changed Paul, it took time for others to believe he had been changed. Paul's reputation had followed him, and it was difficult for people to forget his past: "'Isn't he the man who raised havoc in Jerusalem among those who call on this name? And hasn't he come here to take them as prisoners to the chief priests?' Yet Saul grew more and more powerful and baffled the Jews living in Damascus by proving that Jesus is the Christ" (Acts 9:21-22).

Paul baffled the Jews. You, too, will baffle people when they witness God's transforming power in your life. But it takes time. When you've had a "road to Damascus" experience and God grabs hold of your heart as He grabbed hold of Paul's heart, you'll never be the same again. But it may take time, possibly forever, for others to know of the change that has and is taking place in you.

Be patient and keep your eyes focused on the One who is transforming you daily, taking you from glory to glory. As you learn who you are, what you're about and Who you represent, others will learn who you are, what you're about and Who you represent.

The Apostle Paul said, "As for me, it matters very little how I might be evaluated by you or by any human authority. I don't even trust my own judgment on this point. My conscience is clear, but that doesn't prove I'm right. It is the Lord himself who will examine me and decide"

(1 Corinthians 4:3-4, NLT). In spite of anyone's opinion of your reputation, when all is said and done, you will stand before an audience of One. He is really the only One who counts!

FOR REFLECTION

1. How do I feel about the ways in which I've represented Jesus? Identify my strengths and my weaknesses.

2. Consider some of the primary activities in which I am involved as I humble myself before the Lord. What is my motivation for succeeding in these endeavors?

3. In what ways have I feared man's opinion of me? How have I responded when I didn't receive man's approval? Have I ever had to stand alone, obeying what God has asked of me in spite of not having man's approval? Explain.

4. In what ways have I been a poor representative of Jesus on the earth? As I take time to reflect on this question, do I need to repent before God or man for representing Christ dishonorably?

Reflect on what I am saying, for the Lord will give you insight into all this.
(2 Timothy 2:7)

REPENTANCE

I bow before You with a heavy heart, my God. I've sought after man's approval, Lord Jesus. Fear of man has hindered my obedience to

You. I've tried to justify my reputation when others have falsely accused me or judged me for my past behaviors. Forgive me, God! Forgive me for my poor judgment. Deliver me from fear of man, that I might live only to please You.

OTHER AREAS OF REPENTANCE

Repent, then, and turn to God, so that your sins may be wiped out,
that times of refreshing may come from the Lord.
(Acts 3:19)

SUBMISSION

Father God, I seek Your face today. I want to serve You and You alone. I want Your approval and Your approval alone. You are my God, and I submit myself to You and You alone. Capture my heart as you captured the Apostle Paul's heart. Change me on my road to Damascus, take the scales from my eyes! Fuel my heart with the fire of the Holy Spirit as I seek You with all of my heart. In Jesus' Name.

OTHER AREAS OF SUBMISSION

Submit yourselves, then, to God.
(James 4:7)

FROM THE FATHER'S HEART

My Holy Spirit dwells within you, as We have made Our home in you through My Son. You are the temple of the Holy Spirit, the Spirit of the Living God. You are *in Me*. You are *about Me* and you *represent Me*. Your reputation before man matters not. Follow Me and follow My ways, even if you are of no reputation with man. Because I AM your advocate, you have nothing to fear. Fear of man will prove to be a snare. Fear Me alone.

PERSONAL WORD FROM MY FATHER

Speak, LORD, for your servant is listening.
(1 Samuel 3:9)

DAY 23

MEDITATION

God's Word is truth. It has been forever settled in heaven and will never change. When all else passes away, the solid foundation of His Word will stand. I can trust His promises regardless of what circumstances surround me today. I am not moved by what I see, I am moved by faith. My Father is moved by childlike faith and will move in my environment today, even if my circumstances appear hopeless.

May my meditation be pleasing to him, as I rejoice in the LORD.
(Psalm 104:34)

SCRIPTURE FOCUS

I tell you the truth, anyone who will not receive the kingdom of God like a little child will never enter it.
(Mark 10:15)

What is my Father speaking to me through this Scripture?

DEVOTION FOR THE DAY

Years ago, my husband surprised us with tickets to a Mariners' game. I was thrilled, as our children had never seen a baseball game and I hadn't been to one for many years.

We headed for the old Seattle Kingdome with great expectation in our hearts. While the kids chattered and we found our seats, I overheard some men seated behind us. Listening to their curse- peppered conversation, I wanted to cup my hands over the kids' ears to protect them from the foul language.

How could they talk like that? I sneered to myself. *Especially when there are children right in front of them!*

Trying to be subtle, I twisted around to discover several scruffy men guzzling beer. *Oh boy, we're in for a real treat today*, I grumbled inwardly, turning around stiffly in my seat.

After we stood and sang the national anthem, we watched an astounding fireworks display. The kids were mesmerized by the flair of color and light.

The crowd applauded when the announcer said that they would shoot fireworks every time the Mariners hit a home run. Hoping to witness a continuous colorful blast of fireworks, our expectant children wanted endless home runs.

We settled back into our seats to watch the game. Joe, one-year-old at the time, couldn't sit still, staring curiously at the characters behind us. Amused by the loud men, he shot bright smiles at them through the bottle of juice hanging from his mouth.

Although I attempted to ignore the distractions behind us, the men's obscenities intensified as the game continued. Our irritating neighbors, obviously disgusted with our team's performance, made their opinions clear to anyone within earshot.

I desperately wanted to silence these obnoxious men, but couldn't think of the right words. I silently asked God to give me the proper words. Fuming and keenly aware that the hostile words in my mouth were not from God, I begrudgingly chose to keep my mouth shut.

Inning after inning passed with no score from our team, fueling an even greater display of the men's mounting irritation with the Mariners. As one stood up to shout and shake his fist, his beer toppled over, spilling on his shoes. In disbelief, I watched the beer trickle down to our level, saturating my purse underneath our seats. *Great,* I thought. *What next?*

My husband and our oldest son were enjoying special father/son time, oblivious to the situation causing my blood pressure to skyrocket. Our three-year-old daughter, Emily, dwelling on the fireworks we had seen earlier, was growing impatient and disgruntled. Her patience depleted, she started whining. "I want to see the fireworks, Mommy," she complained, stomping her feet. "I want to see them *right now!*"

"We can't see fireworks until we get a home run," I explained. My words soothed Emily for a moment before she started whining again.

Sitting in my beer soaked environment, frustrated at my less than desirable surroundings, I felt anything but Christian. My patience had worn thin, and I couldn't bear to hear one more complaint from my strong-willed daughter or our drunken neighbors.

Gritting my teeth, I bent down and whispered in Emily's ear. "I *know* you want to see fireworks, but it *won't* happen until our team gets a home run. Why don't you pray and ask God for a home run so you can see your precious fireworks! OK?" Fuming, I didn't care if anyone overheard the angry tone in my parental advice.

Although my suggestion was halfhearted, I felt I had successfully appeased Emily. Now in the ninth inning, I was thankful this negative experience was almost over.

My less than genuine suggestion brightened Emily. Welcoming the idea of asking God for help, she clasped my hands, closed her eyes and prayed. "God, I want to see the fireworks," she said, "and I can't see them unless we get a home run. Please give our team a home run, God.

In Jesus' Name, Amen." Emily nestled back in her seat, satisfied with her prayer and appearing to have settled the fireworks issue.

The next batter from our team stepped up to the plate with two men on base. He swung the bat on the first pitch, slamming a home run over the wall!

A victory cry swept through the stadium. Music blared as the fans cheered wildly. And the fireworks blazed. My mouth dropped open as I watched the batter run the bases. We scored three runs.

Emily bounced up and down like a pogo stick, watching her coveted fireworks. Not the slightest bit surprised, she had made her request known to God, then sat back with no further anxiety, trusting that He would take care of her need. And He did! I, however, having had little faith, now witnessed the result of childlike faith in stunned unbelief.

Childlike faith trusts God without cluttering the mind with reasoning, analysis and doubt. Choose to have childlike faith and watch God slam a home run—even when beer, bad attitudes and whining seem to stand in the way.

FOR REFLECTION

1. Think of a time I witnessed childlike faith in action in my life or in someone else's life. Describe what I witnessed.

2. What does "childlike faith" mean to me? Why do I believe my Father wants me to have childlike faith?

3. What am I facing today that challenges my faith? Explain. What do I need from God today?

4. In relation to question #3, what Biblical promises can I profess as I stand in faith? Record these scriptures and speak them out loud daily. Can I say, "God's Word says it...I believe it...That settles it!" Can I receive God's promises with childlike faith without trying to figure out the details?

Reflect on what I am saying, for the Lord will give you insight into all this.
(2 Timothy 2:7)

REPENTANCE

Everlasting Father, my lack of faith has caused lack in many areas of my life. As I've tried to figure You out, my intellect has gotten in the way of childlike faith. I've put You in a box, unknowingly limiting the areas of which I believed You would want to be involved. In repentance, I demolish those boundaries today and give You access to every part of my life. I open my heart and ask You to cleanse me of my sin of unbelief. I want to be childlike again, Father.

OTHER AREAS OF REPENTANCE

_____

_____

_____

Repent, then, and turn to God, so that your sins may be wiped out,
that times of refreshing may come from the Lord.
(Acts 3:19)

SUBMISSION

O Father, how I love You! I run into Your open arms once again and embrace You as my loving Daddy. Your love astounds me and the mercy

You've shown me, even in my spiritual tantrums, leaves me in awe. I'm grateful that You continue to love me right where I am, and that You respond to me, in spite of my failures and lack of faith. Teach me, Daddy, to walk daily in childlike faith that I might please You. In Jesus' Name.

OTHER AREAS OF SUBMISSION

_____

_____

_____

Submit yourselves, then, to God.
(James 4:7)

FROM THE FATHER'S HEART

I treasure you. You are the apple of My eye! I watch you day and night, always ready to respond to your needs. It gives Me great joy when you come to Me in childlike faith. Do you not know how much it pleases Me to meet your every need? You can call on Me always, in good times and bad. My grace is more than sufficient for you and My power is strongest in your weakness. Lean on Me, My beloved.

PERSONAL WORD FROM MY FATHER

_____

_____

_____

Speak, LORD, for your servant is listening.
(1 Samuel 3:9)

DAY 24

MEDITATION

Everyone, without exception, faces opportunities for offense. When I face an opportunity for offense, I can call out to God for help in extending forgiveness just as Jesus extended me forgiveness when He stretched His arms and was nailed to the cross of Calvary. Through God's grace, He forgave me and now, through God's grace, I choose to forgive others. Though I may never receive an apology for the offenses inflicted on my life, I choose to forgive.

May my meditation be pleasing to him, as I rejoice in the LORD.
(Psalm 104:34)

SCRIPTURE FOCUS

Be kind to each other, tenderhearted, forgiving one another,
just as God through Christ has forgiven you.
(Ephesians 4:32, NLT)

What is my Father speaking to me through this Scripture?

DEVOTION FOR THE DAY

Offense. Some flinch at the word, as it reminds them of the gaping emotional wounds it can leave. Yet facing opportunities for offense is part of God's discipleship package. Conquering the obstacle of offense, a battle won through love and forgiveness, is key to Christian victory.

While responding to offenses, some try to appear as pillars of strength, attempting to convince others that they're unaffected by assaults launched against them. If we remain submitted to God and allow Him to prune us in these tough spots, those assaults can transform us into that pillar of strength we sometimes pretend to be.

When a fellow Christian betrayed me, I tried to keep my emotional pain to myself, knowing that blabbing my business would only make the situation worse. I wasted no time, however, running to God to tattle to my heart's content.

"God, this is *so* wrong," I pleaded. "What should I do?" Whimpering from stinging wounds, I patiently awaited His answer. Expecting God to come to my defense, I hoped He'd let my offender have it with both barrels. I wanted him to suffer as I had suffered. I wanted him punished!

"Forgive him," God whispered.

"What?...But God!" I cried out. "But...but...but...don't You know what he did?"

"Forgive him," He gently repeated.

"But...It isn't fair!" I shrieked in self-defense. "I was wronged!"

"Forgive him," He seemed to whisper again. *"Period."*

After a lengthy spiritual tantrum, I surrendered. Laying my pain at Jesus' feet, I willingly, yet willfully, expressed my choice. "I forgive him, Lord," I said. Taking a deep breath, I added, "Please don't hold this against him." How difficult it was to allow those words to tumble from my mouth!

I didn't feel any better. Memory of the offense soon returned along with the sick feeling in the pit of my stomach. Yet I held fast to my profession of forgiveness every time it came to mind.

Refusing to allow my feelings to rule, the suffered wrong eventually became a faint memory that no longer held me in bondage. The negative emotion vanished and was replaced with compassion and love. Instead of harboring ill feelings, I genuinely asked God to saturate my offender with His unfailing love.

Hurts can linger when offenders won't admit their wrong or if they refuse to apologize. What a news flash to discover that God requires me to forgive even when offenders don't apologize! Apologies are irrelevant in the heavenly school of divine training. God forgave our sin and requires us to forgive others. *Period.*

Ephesians 4:32 instructs us to forgive others just as God through Christ forgave us. God forgave *all* sin, with no exceptions. He forgave it *all* and we must forgive it *all.* God's forgiveness rule has no exceptions.

Jesus shared a sobering truth: "For if you forgive men when they sin against you, your heavenly Father will also forgive you. But if you do not forgive men their sins, your Father will not forgive your sins" (Matthew 6:14-15). If God doesn't forgive us...where does it leave us?

People disappoint. Some spread vicious rumors. Betrayal. Adultery. Deception. Theft. Slander. Gossip. Different hurts, same pain. Offenses sting, *especially* if a fellow Christian inflicted the wound.

It's tempting to plead our case. "But Lord,...he humiliated me... she slandered me...she cheated me... he betrayed me...I just can't forgive!" These words, falling from the lips of wounded people, bring serious consequences.

Regardless of the magnitude of infliction suffered, God requires Christians to forgive. Without divine help, this is a hard pill to swallow. Our loving Father didn't leave us to fend for ourselves though. God poured His love into our hearts by the Holy Spirit. We *can* love and *can* forgive through His love (Romans 5:5).

God in the flesh, Jesus, was a perfect sinless man. He demonstrated selfless, unconditional love, yet those He tried to help sent Him to the cross. Those He came to heal and set free yelled, "Crucify Him!"

Jesus had more reason to refuse to forgive than man will ever have, yet He asked God to forgive those who crucified Him. Jesus knew how to jump the greatest hurdle to forgiveness. He *chose* to walk in forgiveness.

Next time you're the target of an offensive launch, allow God to use it to help you grow in Christian maturity. If you're willing to choose to forgive, God can rub divine Holy Spirit balm on your hurting heart. Ask the Great Physician to help you. His faithful touch will bring healing.

Like flesh wounds, emotional wounds require time to heal. Even after the healing process is complete, memories of offenses won't miraculously disappear, but through God's love, they won't hold you in bondage. Feelings eventually catch up with your confession of forgiveness.

Wounded people, wound people. Hurt people, hurt people. But healed people, heal people and free people, free people! Be healed in Jesus' Name. He'll lift you up, refreshed and ready to fulfill your God-ordained destiny. As you emerge from seasons in the wilderness, leave unforgiveness and offenses behind.

FOR REFLECTION

1. What do I believe will result from my unwillingness to forgive others?

2. Reflecting on a past offense, am I harboring any unforgiveness or bitterness in my heart? Explain. List those that come to mind and talk to God about each one.

3. When others have knowingly or unknowingly harmed me, what has been my response? Is there a pattern to my reaction to offense? What adjustments are needed in my attitude when I face opportunities for offense?

4. Matthew 6:14-15 says, "For if you forgive men when they sin against you, your heavenly Father will also forgive you. But if you do not forgive men their sins, your Father will not forgive your sins." What does this mean to me?

Reflect on what I am saying, for the Lord will give you insight into all this.
(2 Timothy 2:7)

REPENTANCE

God of grace, I fall on my knees and ask Your forgiveness. I've sinned against You and sinned against my brothers and sisters by allowing bitterness and resentment to take hold in my heart. I've refused to forgive those who have sinned against me. I've held them captive and as a result, held myself captive. Today, I choose to forgive. Set the captives free, O God. I free my offenders from the penalty due. I ask You not to hold their sin against them. Forgive me, Father. Forgive my offenders. Cleanse me and make me clean again.

OTHER AREAS OF REPENTANCE

Repent, then, and turn to God, so that your sins may be wiped out,
that times of refreshing may come from the Lord.
(Acts 3:19)

SUBMISSION

Lord Jesus, I've been so selfish in the past, demanding to have my way and being overly sensitive to offenses. I've been defensive when accused. I want my attitude to be like Jesus. I want to have an open heart, always ready to forgive. Just as You have forgiven me, I will forgive others. Father, I release every person who has ever brought me harm and free anyone who may harm me in the future. I choose to forgive them now, Lord. Thank You for the price You paid for the forgiveness of my sin, Lord. Praise Your Holy Name. In Jesus' Name.

OTHER AREAS OF SUBMISSION

_____

_____

_____

Submit yourselves, then, to God.
(James 4:7)

FROM THE FATHER'S HEART

I am pleased with you. The grace you offer in granting forgiveness will release grace in your life. When you set others free, you are setting yourself free. A great price was paid for the forgiveness of your sin and I want you to forgive, always, just as I have forgiven. I offer forgiveness to all and I ask the same of you. Joy will fill you as you walk in the freedom of forgiveness. When you choose forgiveness, you choose life.

PERSONAL WORD FROM MY FATHER

Speak, LORD, for your servant is listening.
(1 Samuel 3:9)

DAY 25

MEDITATION

I hear the voice of the Good Shepherd and I know His voice. The devil tempts me to question my ability to hear God's voice and causes me to doubt the ways in which God speaks to my heart. I can trust the voice of the Holy Spirit, who will always lead me into all truth. God's voice and leading will never contradict His Word, but will align with His Word. His Word is truth! I am dependent on God, not on man.

May my meditation be pleasing to him, as I rejoice in the LORD.
(Psalm 104:34)

SCRIPTURE FOCUS

"I am the LORD; that is my name!
I will not give my glory to another or my praise to idols."
(Isaiah 42:8)

What is my Father speaking to me through this Scripture?

....

....

....

DEVOTION FOR THE DAY

"*THIS* is my Son, whom I love. Listen to *HIM!*"

The Mount of Transfiguration appeared suddenly in my living room on an otherwise normal morning, accompanying ten words that to this day, ring loud in my spirit. Though I don't remember if my eyes were open or closed, I saw Peter, James and John gazing at the wondrous sight of Jesus shining brighter than the noonday sun, His clothes whiter than an earthly launderer could possibly make them.

Seeing Moses and Elijah with Jesus, Peter, who sometimes jumps into action before he's in the right gear, said, "It's good that you're all here! Whooppieee! Let's build a tabernacle for each of you!" Although I couldn't tell if Peter's exuberant response resulted from awe of God or fear of God, the sobering words that followed didn't leave much room for question.

A cloud enveloped them, and the voice of God spoke from the cloud: "**THIS** is My Son in whom I am well pleased. Listen to **HIM**." The disciples fell on their face in fear. But Jesus touched them, saying, "Do not be afraid." And when they looked up, Moses and Elijah were gone, leaving only Jesus.

In awe myself, I heard again, "**THIS** is My Son in whom I am well pleased. Listen to **HIM**." The loving, yet stern command arrived in my home and my heart, bringing correction, yet peace.

I thought of the righteous anger Jesus demonstrated when He cleared the Temple where they were selling animals for sacrifices, turning His house of prayer into a den of thieves (Luke 19:45).

In the vision of the Mount of Transfiguration, God seemed righteously angry. And it's no wonder.

The body of Christ has elevated pastors and other spiritual leaders to a place equal and even above the Son of God. In search of direction for their lives, God's people seek spiritual leaders for answers instead of seeking Him. God is jealous for His people and wants no other before Him.

I had been guilty of putting others before God too. Many times. I remembered the bittersweet day we received news that our unmarried son was going to be a father, making us grandparents for the first time. I immediately made an appointment with my pastor. While God, the One who knew every detail and had all of the answers I needed, came in a close second. Sadly, sometimes I sought God as a last resort or afterthought.

Kneeling on the carpet in the living room, I bowed down to God in repentance, realizing that I had made idols out of man, putting greater significance on my spiritual leaders than I had God. "Father, forgive me!" I cried. "Forgive us for making idols out of our leaders."

We need the spiritual leaders God gave to the body of Christ as gifts. The Apostle Paul tells us that God gave, "some to be apostles, some to be prophets, some to be evangelists, and some to be pastors and teachers, to *prepare God's people for works of service,* so that the body of Christ may be built up until we all reach unity in the faith and in the knowledge of the Son of God and become mature, attaining to the whole measure of the fullness of Christ" (Ephesians 4:11-13). These ministry gifts equip the body of Christ for ministry, but are not responsible for changing the body of Christ. That is God's job alone.

Although seeking counsel from spiritual leaders is wise, those leaders were not intended to become a substitute for God. He detests idols, which are not all cast from gold, metal, stone or clay. Some idols, created by man, *are* man.

God's people often depend more on man's direction than on God's direction, even bowing down to them in worship. We must cleanse the temple of the idols of man, as they are detestable in God's sight!

Woe to the spiritual leaders who lust after being placed on a pedestal, leading God's sheep to themselves instead of to the one true God. Woe to those who willingly make themselves the source of man's idolatry. Woe to the shepherds who spiritually abuse God's sheep, misusing scripture to shame them into submission to them. God is breaking His people free from this bondage, so they can be free to worship Him alone.

God our Father, the Good Shepherd, cares for His sheep. The Good Shepherd has given us the ability through the power of the Holy Spirit to hear and follow His voice (John 10:27). The Good Shepherd gave the gift of the Holy Spirit as our Counselor, Friend, Comforter, Helper, Advocate, and Teacher. The Spirit of the Living God dwells within each believer, leading them and guiding them into all truth.

God desires for you to grow up, becoming mature, attaining the whole measure of the fullness of Christ. As the Father said on the Mount of Transfiguration, He says to you this day: *THIS* is My Son whom I love. Listen to *HIM*.

Forgive us, Lord, for erecting idols of man. Cleanse our temples where we have allowed man to rob You of Your praise. We bow down in worship as we have heard Your words: *THIS* is My Son whom I love. Listen to *HIM*. Yes, Lord! When we lift our eyes to the heavens, we will gaze only upon You and Your wondrous beauty.

FOR REFLECTION

1. How does God speak to me? Do I believe that my Father speaks to me or do I believe He speaks to others only? Explain.

2. To whom do I go when I need answers or counsel? What motivates me to seek them? Have I been required to get my spiritual leader's approval?

3. Does God speak to me through His written Word? Give an example. Does God speak to me through other people? Give an example. Does God speak to me through circumstances? Give an example.

4. Do I rely on my spiritual leaders more or less than I rely on God? Do I need the approval of my spiritual leaders to obey the direction which God is giving me? Why?

Reflect on what I am saying, for the Lord will give you insight into all this.
(2 Timothy 2:7)

REPENTANCE

My God, I have sinned against You! I've erected idols out of man, putting my faith in them instead of You. I've put man on a pedestal, seeking man's direction, though You are the only one with the master plan for my life. Forgive me, Lord, of the sin of idolatry! I'm sorry for following man's voice instead of following Your voice. I demolish my idols today, Lord God, and lift You up. You and You alone, shall I follow.

OTHER AREAS OF REPENTANCE

Repent, then, and turn to God, so that your sins may be wiped out, that times of refreshing may come from the Lord.
(Acts 3:19)

SUBMISSION

Father God, Jesus is Your beloved Son and My Lord and Savior. I shall listen to Him. I place my life under His authority and ask You to open my ears wide to hear His voice with clarity. I trust that You will lead me and guide me by Your Spirit, keeping me on the path which You have ordained. I love You, Lord, with all of my heart, body, soul and strength. As I walk with You, transform me, mold me and make me into a vessel to bring You glory, honor and praise. In Jesus' Name.

OTHER AREAS OF SUBMISSION

_____

_____

_____

Submit yourselves, then, to God.
(James 4:7)

FROM THE FATHER'S HEART

I am pleased with My Son. Listen to Him. Follow Him. Many voices rally for your attention, trying to speak into your life, but you must silence other voices to hear My Son's voice clearly. As you follow Him and walk in His ways, you will experience the abundant life for which I've made provision. Everything you need is in My Son and everything you need to become is in My Son. Abide in Me and My Son. We shall walk together beside the still waters where you will find peace.

PERSONAL WORD FROM MY FATHER

_____

_____

_____

Speak, LORD, for your servant is listening.
(1 Samuel 3:9)

DAY 26

MEDITATION

God is at work in my life, even in the midst of my ever-changing circumstances. Regardless of what I face today, God is present in the details, even when I don't realize it. I choose to put on Christ daily, demonstrating a Christlike attitude in the midst of suffering. I can bring hope to others as I radiate the joy of the Lord in spite of my circumstances. As I reach out to bring joy to others, I myself will be blessed.

May my meditation be pleasing to him, as I rejoice in the LORD.
(Psalm 104:34)

SCRIPTURE FOCUS

For I have learned to be content whatever the circumstances. I know what it is to be in need, and I know what it is to have plenty. I have learned the secret of being content in any and every situation, whether well fed or hungry, whether living in plenty or in want. I can do everything through him who gives me strength.
(Philippians 4:11-13)

What is my Father speaking to me through this Scripture?

_____

_____

_____

DEVOTION FOR THE DAY

"Would you consider volunteering with me at the nursing home, Mom?" our daughter asked. She delivered her proposition with hesitance, as she knew that my plate already overflowed with commitments. Though wanting to earn extra credit during her first college semester, she preferred not to volunteer alone, especially at a nursing home, where she might encounter uncomfortable situations.

I welcomed the opportunity without giving it a second thought, not only because I love elderly people, but because I wanted to spend time with Emily. Since she moved to the dorm only six miles from our home, I had missed her greatly. She wasn't only my daughter, but had become a friend, prayer partner, exercise buddy and confidant.

I jumped on the opportunity to volunteer. Little did Emily or I know, however, that God, the Supreme Volunteer Coordinator, had orchestrated our work at the nursing home. Though we intended to bless the residents, God intended to bless us beyond understanding.

After receiving basic instruction and taking a facility tour, the volunteer coordinator shared various options for how we might fill our volunteer hours. Hearing about Betty, who loved to play Scrabble, both of our hearts leaped. Mom, who had passed away in '98, was referred to as the Scrabble Queen of Hopkins, where I was raised. With countless memories of playing Scrabble with Mom, Emily and I welcomed the opportunity to play Scrabble with our new friend.

The coordinator led us to Betty's room and made introductions. Betty, born with cerebral palsy, was wheelchair bound and now also suffered with Lou Gehrig's disease. Oxygen helped her breathe easier.

Although Betty's speech difficulty made us wonder if she might be mentally challenged, we soon learned that she was not only highly intelligent, but had a delightful sense of humor. Betty's complex words and winning Scrabble scores testified to her sharp intellect. Though she needed a helping hand in placing tiles on the board, she needed no help in creating high scoring words.

Because of the progressing disease, Betty's body didn't cooperate very well with her mind. She understood everything people said, but had to patiently wait for her body to cooperate in communicating what was in her mind.

Over the next months, I habitually asked the Lord to enable us to understand Betty. He answered that prayer. And when at first we didn't understand, Betty lovingly and patiently repeated herself until we did understand.

Full of the joy of the Lord, Betty glowed with the love of Jesus. In spite of her condition, she never complained. Not once. I sensed the conviction of the Holy Spirit as I observed Betty's resolve to remain pleasant in her circumstances, remembering how often I complained, even about having a bad hair day!

As Betty tootled back to her room in her electric wheelchair, she seemed like a mother hen, on the lookout for other residents who might be in need. Her genuine care and concern for others followed her everywhere her wheelchair took her.

We learned more about Betty's life as we played Scrabble. She had been married to Kent, who also had cerebral palsy, for 37 years, until his death in 1994. Kent had the athetoid type of CP, which gave him little or no control over his limbs, which wriggled and thrashed around by themselves while he sat powerless in his wheelchair. He only had some control over his feet and toes, which enabled him to lie on his back and dial a radio program or a phone number. He could also turn the pages of a book with a pencil held in his teeth.

Betty, who could still walk at that time, lovingly and selflessly cared for Kent daily, feeding him, dressing him and taking him everywhere he wanted to go. Kent, a remarkable man, in spite of his extreme physical limitations, had written countless magazine articles, touched lives around the globe and was the main driver for the approval and installation of wheelchair ramps in the city of Spokane. Betty, his helpmate, was key to all Kent accomplished through their life together, the humble servant behind the scenes who never took credit or praise for anything.

Possessing a key that the Apostle Paul had discovered, Betty knew what it was like to live with challenging circumstances. But she had learned to be content in all things, knowing that she can do all things through Christ who strengthens her.

Though Emily and I intended to bless others at the nursing home, we ourselves were blessed and enriched by Betty, one of my greatest heroes. We still play Scrabble, but I no longer complain about bad hair days!

FOR REFLECTION

1. Have I ever witnessed someone like Betty, who daily faces significant challenges, yet maintains a joyful spirit? How would I describe that person?

2. Make contact with the person identified in the previous question. Tell him/her what I've observed and share the impact it's had on my life. Ask him/her to share his/her testimony with me.

3. What physical, spiritual or emotional challenges do I face daily? What has been my attitude about these challenges?

4. In relation to the challenges listed in the previous question, what can I do to help someone else in need? May the Holy Spirit direct me to someone I might bless and reveal how I might bless him/her.

Reflect on what I am saying, for the Lord will give you insight into all this.
(2 Timothy 2:7)

REPENTANCE

Oh God, my God. I put on sackcloth and ashes in repentance. Forgive me for my sin! Though You have blessed me abundantly, I've complained and moaned like a stubborn brat. I've been ungrateful and focused on my suffering instead of being focused on You. I've magnified my problems instead of magnifying You. I need Your mercy once again, Lord. Forgive me!

OTHER AREAS OF REPENTANCE

Repent, then, and turn to God, so that your sins may be wiped out, that times of refreshing may come from the Lord.
(Acts 3:19)

SUBMISSION

Dear God, although I want what You want, I'm so very weak. Strengthen me for the journey. Strengthen me by Your Spirit in my inner being that I might stand strong in the face of trial. You've blessed me abundantly, O Lord, and I thank You! I surrender to You in the midst of my suffering. Have Your way in me. I trust You to complete the good work You've started in me. My heart belongs to You, my Lord and my God. In Jesus' Name.

OTHER AREAS OF SUBMISSION

Submit yourselves, then, to God.
(James 4:7)

FROM THE FATHER'S HEART

I love you, my little lamb. You are precious in My sight, even when you feel you've failed Me. I love you where you are right now and I will always love you. My love is unconditional and is not dependant on your actions or your faith. My love is unconditional and unchanging. I am your Father. I care for you and love you. Stop striving for My love. My love is yours. Embrace it now.

PERSONAL WORD FROM MY FATHER

Speak, LORD, for your servant is listening.
(1 Samuel 3:9)

DAY 27

MEDITATION

My dream was in my Father's heart long before He put it in my heart and only He knows the details of when and how it will be fulfilled. The dream He breathed into my spirit will come to pass, regardless of what others have told me. My Father will prepare me, train me and raise me up to fulfill my dream in His perfect timing. Not before its time, not after its time, but right on time!

May my meditation be pleasing to him, as I rejoice in the LORD.
(Psalm 104:34)

SCRIPTURE FOCUS

You intended to harm me, but God intended it all for good.
He brought me to this position so I could save the lives of many people.
(Genesis 50:20, NLT)

What is my Father speaking to me through this Scripture?

DEVOTION FOR THE DAY

It's a good thing I'm not God. I would only allow evil people to suffer and would spare good people from all suffering. God doesn't agree.

Joseph, a patriarch of the 12 tribes of Israel, experienced more than his share of suffering. And it didn't seem fair. It wasn't Joseph's fault that his father, Jacob, favored him, being the first born of his beloved wife Rachel. His brothers raged with jealously because of the favoritism Joseph received as Daddy's pet.

Because of his brothers' hatred, Joseph, at age 17, received a hostile response when he shared his dreams, in which his brothers bowed down to him. The very suggestion of Joseph reigning over them further fueled the brothers' jealousy.

Joseph's siblings saw an opportune moment to retaliate when their father sent Joseph to check on them as they were pasturing Jacob's flocks. Seeing Joseph headed their way, they schemed their despised brother's demise. "Here comes that dreamer!" they said, wanting to kill him (Genesis 37:19).

Instead of killing Joseph, they tossed him in a pit, then stopped for a lunch break! Joseph's problems didn't end there though, as they pulled him from the pit, and then sold him into slavery. Back on the ranch, they lied to their father Jacob, telling him that a wild animal had Joseph for snack.

The dreams Joseph had shared would be a long time in coming. It didn't seem fair.

Now in slavery, Joseph entered the service of Potiphar, an Egyptian officer and captain of the guard for Pharaoh, king of Egypt. He remained faithful as a slave, honoring his master in every way possible. Yet Joseph was slapped with an unfair prison sentence after being falsely accused of rape by Potiphar's wife.

It didn't seem fair. Joseph had resisted the woman's persistent advances and didn't even consider dishonoring his master by sleeping with his wife, even when she repeatedly pressured him to do so. Joseph had remained honorable before God and man only to find himself not only tossed in a pit, but also tossed into prison.

While in jail, Joseph remained a faithful servant. He interpreted dreams for the king's cupbearer and baker, who were also imprisoned, revealing correctly that the baker would die and the cupbearer's position would be restored. Though the cupbearer enjoyed his new freedom, he quickly forgot about Joseph, leaving him in prison where he spent two more years. It didn't seem fair.

But the day arrived when Joseph's gift of dream interpretation was needed again. Pharaoh, who had two dreams of his own, was desperate to know what they meant. Remembering how Joseph had accurately interpreted his dream, the king's cupbearer recommended Joseph's services.

Seeing Joseph's impressive wisdom, the Pharaoh not only freed him from prison, but also gave him charge of his kingdom, second only to the Pharaoh himself. Now 30, it had been 13 long years since God had given Joseph his dreams.

Nine years later, at age 39, Joseph, now powerful governor of Egypt, came face to face with his brothers who had sold him into slavery. His brothers bowed low before him, just as Joseph had seen in his dreams 22 years earlier.

The story of Joseph doesn't seem fair. But God does not agree with our assessment, nor does Joseph. Instead of being bitter, Joseph offered his brothers grace and forgiveness, saying, *"You intended to harm me, but God intended it all for good. He brought me to this position so I could save the lives of many people"* (Genesis 50:20, NLT).

Has God given you a dream? Those God-given dreams, although full of divine purpose, rarely come to pass immediately, and rarely do they come to pass without much trial and tribulation.

We, like Joseph, must endure our proving ground where God tests and trains us in preparation for the fulfillment of the very dreams He put in our hearts. As our preparation unfolds, circumstances often don't seem fair. But God in His great wisdom, knows how to train us, allowing suffering even when we're honorable before Him, doing everything we know to do.

The dreams God gave Joseph as a teenager didn't come to pass until he was a grown man. Joseph did not complain his way through those years of preparation, but remained faithful wherever God put him, and God blessed him throughout the process. Maturing and growing through each training place, Joseph squeezed everything he could out of each experience through which he walked.

Although we might want to go from point A to point Z overnight to fulfill our God-given dreams, we must allow God to take us from point A to point B, then from point B to point C in His timing. At each step along the way, if we remain teachable, we will grow and mature while God prepares us for the fulfillment of our dreams.

I suspect if God gave us a glimpse of what awaited at point Z we'd be petrified, as we simply would not be prepared for it. God prepares us for our destiny through much needed, divine, on-going on the job training.

Although it may not require 22 years for God's dream to be fulfilled in you, as it did Joseph, don't be in a rush to move on. Squeeze everything you can out of the place God has you right now, even when it doesn't seem fair. He will move you on in His perfect timing.

FOR REFLECTION

I. Describe the dream God has given me. When and how did He give me this dream?

2. What has happened since I received this dream? Have I faced anything that challenges my dream or has its fulfillment come to pass without opposition?

3. Have I shared my God-given dreams with others? If so, what was their response? Do they support my dream or do they laugh at it? How has another's response affected my feelings about God's dream? Have I allowed others to kill my dream?

4. Have I come into agreement with and submitted myself to God's plan where my dream is concerned? Have I, like the Virgin Mary, said, "Be it unto Me according to what You have said?" Am I willing to allow my Father to bring my dream to pass in spite of the fact that it may seem impossible to me?

Reflect on what I am saying, for the Lord will give you insight into all this.
(2 Timothy 2:7)

REPENTANCE

Mighty God, I've doubted the dream You conceived in my spirit. I've questioned what You've shown me and have wondered how it could possibly come to pass. I feel so unworthy to be used of You, God. Change my heart, Lord God. I'm sorry for questioning that which You've shown me and ask You to forgive me for rejecting what I believe You gave me. Forgive me for my wavering faith, Lord. I'm sorry, Father. I can do nothing without You, but my dream is possible with You.

Other areas of repentance

....

....

....

Repent, then, and turn to God, so that your sins may be wiped out,
that times of refreshing may come from the Lord.
(Acts 3:19)

SUBMISSION

God, You are the King of kings and Lord of lords! You are the author
and the finisher of my faith. I submit myself to Your divinely orchestrated preparation and know that Your plan is for my good and for Your
glory. I willingly submit to You, and trust You to make my dream
become a reality. Breathe life into that which appears dead. Be it unto
me according to what You have said. In Jesus' Name.

Other areas of submission

....

....

....

Submit yourselves, then, to God.
(James 4:7)

FROM THE FATHER'S HEART

The dream I conceived in your spiritual womb is part of My sovereign plan in the earth. Embrace the dream, as you are My chosen vessel
to birth that which will make My Name great. Without Me, you can do
nothing. Without Me, the dream would surely die. But with Me, it will

come to pass gloriously. I will do it. I, the Giver of Life, will breathe life into others through the life I've breathed into you.

PERSONAL WORD FROM MY FATHER

_____

_____

_____

Speak, LORD, for your servant is listening.
(1 Samuel 3:9)

DAY 28

MEDITATION

Angels are part of God's wondrous creation, sent to serve and protect God's people. Though I may not see them in the natural realm, they have existed since the beginning and will be present at the end of the age. Although I do not worship angels, I thank God for them and embrace opportunities to see them in action.

May my meditation be pleasing to him, as I rejoice in the LORD.
(Psalm 104:34)

SCRIPTURE FOCUS

Praise the LORD, you his angels, you mighty ones
who do his bidding, who obey his word. Praise the LORD,
all his heavenly hosts, you his servants who do his will.
(Psalm 103:20-21)

What is my Father speaking to me through this Scripture?

DEVOTION FOR THE DAY

I love angels. After collecting and receiving angel figures as gifts throughout my life, they grace every room in my home. God's mighty angels fill my home, too.

Angels have played a key role since the beginning of time, present at key events throughout scripture from Genesis to Revelation. People saw angels. They talked to angels. Nowhere in scripture does God wipe angels off the face of the earth, the heavens or anywhere else. Angels, in fact, are present today, being used as messengers of God to serve those who will inherit salvation (Hebrews 1:14).

When my daughter, Emily, was a toddler, I saw the work of an angel before my eyes. Arriving at the grocery store parking lot, I took Emily out of her car seat and set her down next to the van. While glancing away, I grabbed the sliding van door, gave it a good pull, and swung it shut as I always did.

The door, though, stopped short from closing. When I didn't hear the door slam shut, I looked down. I gasped when I saw that Emily had rested her hand inside the door latch. Had the door shut, her little hand would surely have been crushed. An unseen angel had stepped in to stop that door. God used his angel to protect Emily from harm, as it says in Psalm 91:11, "For he will command his angels concerning you to guard you in all your ways."

As seen in our key verse for today, angels do God's bidding and obey His Word. They act *only* in line with God's Word. The angels play a key role in doing God's bidding, but we play a key role in enabling them to carry out those instructions. We must speak in agreement with God's Word, as angels can respond only to His Word.

Picture it! Seeing a growing pile of bills while our checkbook balance shrinks, we say, "God, in spite of how things look, I thank You for meeting all of my needs according to Your glorious riches in Christ Jesus!" (Philippians 4:19.) Off they go as God sends His angels on an assignment, going to and fro bringing in the finances you need.

But then, taking a second look at the bottom line, you lose hope. "There's no way I'll ever make ends meet. It's never going to work out." Our words, contradicting God's Word, bring the angels on assignment to a screeching halt, as they can act *only* in response to God's Word.

Speaking in agreement with the Word of God creates an environment for angels to fulfill their heavenly assignments in our lives. I wonder how often our misguided words trip up the angels.

The spiritual realm in which angels abide, is real. God can pull back the curtain to the spiritual world as He wills, showing us what might otherwise be hidden from us.

The prophet Elisha asked God to pull the curtain back long ago, and God did! (2 Kings 6:9-18.) When the King of Aram sent horses, chariots and a strong force to surround the city where Elisha and his servant were staying, Elisha's servant became terrified. But Elisha, who had no fear, said, "Don't be afraid. Those who are with us are more than those who are with them." Then Elisha prayed, "O Lord, open his eyes so he may see." The Lord opened the servant's eyes, enabling him to see the hills full of horses and chariots of fire all around Elisha.

Open our eyes, Lord! As you grow in the knowledge of God's Word and establish His will according to His Word, speak in agreement with that Word. Speaking God's Word will not only build the framework for your tomorrows, but will create an atmosphere for the heavenly messengers to fulfill their assignments. And you just might even see them at work!

FOR REFLECTION

1. Do I believe that angels exist? Why or why not? Look up Hebrews 1:14 and memorize it this week. What does this scripture mean to me?

2. Have I experienced an angelic visitation or supernatural protection that cannot be explained in the natural realm? Do I know someone who has witnessed an angelic intervention? Share the experience.

3. Pay close attention to my words today. Am I speaking in line with God's Word, positioning myself for angelic intervention or am I speaking contrary to God's Word, bringing God's angels to a screeching stop?

4. Spend time in praise and thanksgiving for God's protection through angelic beings. Purpose to speak in agreement with God's Word and ask a family member to hold me accountable.

Reflect on what I am saying, for the Lord will give you insight into all this.
(2 Timothy 2:7)

REPENTANCE

God of all creation, instead of being in wonder of Your wondrous mysteries, I've often doubted them. I'm sorry for the ways I've questioned the things I do not understand. At times I seem limited in my humanness, believing only what I can see. Forgive me, Father, for I have sinned. Forgive me, Father, for speaking words contrary to your Word instead of speaking the truth of Your Word to which Your angels hearken.

OTHER AREAS OF REPENTANCE

_Repent, then, and turn to God, so that your sins may be wiped out,
that times of refreshing may come from the Lord._
(Acts 3:19)

SUBMISSION

Father God, You are so good to me. Thank You for releasing guardian angels who hearken to Your voice to protect and serve me, even when I'm not aware of their presence. I surrender my tongue to You, Father; take control of my mouth. Enable me, Lord, to speak only words that are in agreement with Your Holy Word. May I hearken to Your voice and speak Your Word so Your angels can hearken to Your voice and act upon Your Word to bring Your divine plan to pass. In Jesus' Name.

OTHER AREAS OF SUBMISSION

Submit yourselves, then, to God.
(James 4:7)

FROM THE FATHER'S HEART

I AM watching over you always, My faithful servant. I guard your ways and protect your path, even when you are unaware. My angels are

round about you always, listening to My commands and responding to My voice. I want you, My child, to listen to My commands and respond to My voice too. As you listen to Me and walk in My ways, I will open your spiritual eyes even wider to witness and proclaim the wondrous work of My hand.

PERSONAL WORD FROM MY FATHER

_____

_____

_____

Speak, LORD, for your servant is listening.
(1 Samuel 3:9)

DAY 29

MEDITATION

My wise Father blessed me with the privilege of choosing the people with whom I develop a relationship. I am influenced by my relationships and my relationship with others influences them. God does not require me to engage in a relationship with everyone who crosses my path. As I seek wisdom from my Father, He will help me establish the relationships He desires, to fulfill His purpose.

May my meditation be pleasing to him, as I rejoice in the LORD.
(Psalm 104:34)

SCRIPTURE FOCUS

Make allowance for each other's faults, and forgive anyone who offends you. Remember, the Lord forgave you, so you must forgive others.
(Colossians 3:13, NLT)

What is my Father speaking to me through this Scripture?

DEVOTION FOR THE DAY

I cherished our nightly bedtime routine as a young mother, as it created tender memories that I still ponder to this day.

One evening while tucking our youngest son, Joe, into bed, he rattled off a lengthy but heartfelt prayer. "And God," he said at the end, "give everyone in the whole wide world a good sleep tonight...except for the bad guys." God surely has a sense of humor!

Before switching the lights off, I turned back to him. "Mom," Joe said, as I planted a kiss on his cherub-like cheek, "do I have to like everyone?"

"Well, of course you do!" I said. "We're supposed to love others, even our enemies."

"I'm not talking about *love*," he said, determined to help me understand. "*Like. Like.* I'm talking about *like*, Mom, not *love*."

"Oh," I sighed.

Sitting on the edge of Joe's bed, I pondered his question while he stared at me with expectation.

"If we know God, which we do," I told him, "we'll love others because God is love." Joe was far from satisfied.

"I *know* God wants us to *love* other people, Mom. But I'm not talking about that!" His frustration at my inability to understand or answer his question mounted. "I'm talking about *liking* people. Do I have to *like* everyone?"

"Let's see," I paused. "What happens when you like someone?"

"That's easy," he said, "when I like someone, I want to be his friend. I want to spend time with him and play with him." Still thinking, he added, "I like to be around people I like."

"And what happens when you don't like someone?" I asked.

"I don't want to be friends with someone I don't like. I don't want to play with him because I feel bad when I'm around him." Contemplating his answer, he continued. "Some people aren't very nice, Mom. They're mean and they don't even care."

What a dilemma for my young son.

Does God require us to like everyone?

It's natural to like those who are kind, loving and generous. It's easy to like people who are like us, who share our interests, and have common goals. It's also easy to like people who fall into the "easy to like" category. It's not easy however, to like, or to love, those who are unkind, unloving and selfish.

The Bible never mentions a requirement to like everyone. In fact, God is silent on the subject. God doesn't require us to befriend every person who crosses our path either. He gives us the great privilege of choosing with whom we want to cultivate friendships and with whom we choose to spend our time.

Although God doesn't require us to like everyone, He is undeniably clear on the subject of love. Christians must love others, regardless of how awful their behavior is or how short they fall from our expectations. Whether one is easy to love or difficult to love, we must love others with the love God poured into our hearts by the Holy Spirit (Romans 5:5). Without God's divine love dwelling within us, loving the unlovable is a hard pill to swallow.

We may meet people we don't particularly like for one reason or another, just as some people may not like us for one reason or another. Whether or not we like all people, God requires us to love them.

"Liking or not liking people is just a personal feeling," I told Joe as our conversation wound down. "It's sort of irrelevant. But loving people is a choice we make based on God's command to love others as He loves us." Grabbing my Bible, I opened to a well-worn page. "Second John 6 says, 'His command is that you walk in love.'"

"Well, Joe," I said. "It looks like God wants us to walk in love, but we don't have to walk in like."

Closing his eyes, Joe ended his prayer. "P.S. Thanks God, that I don't have to like mean guys and I don't have to be their best friend."

"Yes, Lord, thank You for that," I added. "And for the wisdom to know the difference."

FOR REFLECTION

1. From my perspective, what is the difference between "love" and "like"?

2. As I think of someone I like, why do I like him/her? As I think of someone I don't like, why don't I like him/her?

3. Are there any people in my circle of relationships with whom I've felt obligated to maintain a relationship, yet it seems to be a constant struggle to maintain that relationship?

4. As I examine my circle of friends, how much time am I investing in these relationships? Is the effort I'm putting into these relationships producing fruitful results? If not, what is being produced in these relationships?

Reflect on what I am saying, for the Lord will give you insight into all this.
(2 Timothy 2:7)

REPENTANCE

O God, You have opened my eyes today. I've made poor choices in relationships and misinterpreted Your desire for me to forgive. I see now that although You require me to forgive those who have sinned against me, You don't require me to continue a relationship with those who bring me harm. I'm sorry for my failings. Forgive me for my sin, Lord God. Forgive me for my ignorance and poor judgment. Thank You, Father, for the blood of Your Son, shed for the forgiveness of sin. Cleanse me now, loving Father, from my sin.

OTHER AREAS OF REPENTANCE

Repent, then, and turn to God, so that your sins may be wiped out,
that times of refreshing may come from the Lord.
(Acts 3:19)

SUBMISSION

Here I am, Holy Lord. I want You to have Your way in every area of my life. I bring to You all of my relationships. I lay them before You now and ask that You would establish those relationships that are built on Your purpose, those that will draw me closer to You. I give You permission to remove relationships that might take me away from You or hinder Your purpose in my life. Thank You God, for the privilege of choosing relationships. Please choose my relationships for me, dear Lord. In Jesus' Name.

OTHER AREAS OF SUBMISSION

Submit yourselves, then, to God.
(James 4:7)

FROM THE FATHER'S HEART

I love you with My unfailing love and want you to love others. I have poured My love into your heart by My Holy Spirit and you shall pour out that love to others. I forgave you through the shed blood of My Beloved Son, and I want you to pour out My forgiveness to others, even those you do not like. I shall establish the relationships ordained of Me and will send the roots down deep so you can grow and flourish in Me. Make Me the center of your relationships and I shall lead and guide you to great abundance.

PERSONAL WORD FROM MY FATHER

Speak, LORD, for your servant is listening.
(1 Samuel 3:9)

DAY 30

MEDITATION

Although I will face many opportunities for suffering, I can choose to trust God in the midst of suffering, knowing that He has a perfectly orchestrated plan. For the joy set before Him, He endured the cross for me. For the joy set before me, I will endure my seasons of suffering for the good of others and for God's glory, even when I don't understand.

May my meditation be pleasing to him, as I rejoice in the LORD.
(Psalm 104:34)

SCRIPTURE FOCUS

"Now my heart is troubled, and what shall I say?
'Father, save me from this hour'?
No, it was for this very reason I came to this hour.
(John 12:27)

What is my Father speaking to me through this Scripture?

DEVOTION FOR THE DAY

As a little girl, I used to stare at the cross hanging at the front of the church where I was raised. Seeing the crown of thorns pressed into Jesus' head gripped my young soul. Intense compassion pierced my heart when I noticed the spikes that had been pounded through His hands and feet, and the blood flowing from His body.

While church services continued, I remained lost in thought, still gazing at Jesus' lifeless body. I didn't understand; it didn't make sense. I had heard Bible stories of Jesus healing and helping people. Although I didn't know Jesus personally, I liked Him. I liked Him a lot. I knew He was a good man, so His suffering and gruesome death bothered me. It bothered me a lot.

Picturing the Roman soldiers spitting on Jesus and beating Him with no regret angered me. It sickened me to think of Pilate's regiment flogging His back repeatedly with a lead-tipped whip until He was unrecognizable. Those who stripped Him, humiliated and mocked Him, I felt must be punished with the maximum sentence. With every slap, every nail, every flogging, and every curse, I wanted to see payback. But most of all, I wished that I could have saved Jesus from suffering at all.

Peter didn't want Jesus to suffer either (Matthew 16:21-23). After hearing Jesus foretell His coming death, Peter said, "Heaven forbid, Lord! This will never happen to you." Peter's words brought a stern rebuke from Jesus. Peter, the Lord said, was seeing things merely from a human point of view, not from God's view (Matthew 16:23).

Although Peter and I had good intentions—wanting to save Jesus from suffering—Jesus knew it was for this very reason that He left His heavenly dwelling to come to earth as Son of God and Son of man. He came to suffer and die, fulfilling His Father's divine plan. In spite of wicked men who plotted against Jesus and put Him to death, God would accomplish salvation for man by raising His Son from the dead.

I wonder if Satan might have grinned ear to pointy ear when he saw Jesus suffer and take His last breath. Though thinking he had won the victory, little did he know that Christ's suffering and death was part of God's plan to disarm him, and make a public spectacle of him when Jesus triumphed over him *through* the cross (Colossians 2:15).

Three days after hearing Jesus say, "It is finished," Satan likely realized *he* was finished. If Satan had known that Jesus' suffering and death would bring salvation to man, he likely would wish he could go back to the drawing board!

Though I felt disdain for the men who inflicted Jesus' pain, suffering and death, God used them as tools to carry out His plan. If Jesus had not been crucified or died, He could not have risen from the dead, victorious over sin and death. Without His suffering, we would have no hope. But *through* His suffering, we have hope. *Through* His suffering we have life eternal!

We, too, will suffer. Jesus, knowing His followers would face seasons of suffering as He did, didn't ask His Father to deliver them *from* the trial, but instead asked Him to strengthen them *in* the trial. After telling Peter that Satan wanted to sift him like wheat, Jesus assured him that He had already prayed for him, that *his faith would not fail him* (Luke 22:31-32). Jesus looks at suffering from God's perspective, not man's perspective.

As we witness others in seasons of suffering, may we keep God's perspective, remembering that He has a plan that often includes suffering. Instead of asking God to deliver them from the trial, may we plead in prayer that as they walk *through* the trial, their faith will not fail them. Let's hope others pray the same for us!

Have you been confronted by "Roman soldiers" whose goal in life is to see your demise? Have you faced enemies, seen and unseen, who are set on seeing you fail? God is well aware that your enemies have you in their sights. But, like those who crucified Christ, they are mere pawns in God's hands, key tools used for His divinely orchestrated plan. As you walk *through* your season of suffering, may you find God's perspective so you bring life to others.

FOR REFLECTION

1. As I picture the suffering Jesus endured on the cross of Calvary, what does His crucifixion, death and resurrection mean to me? What does the statement, "For the joy set before Him, He endured the cross" mean to me?

2. Have I ever been desperate for deliverance from my physical, emotional or spiritual suffering? What resulted from my suffering? Have I wondered why I had to endure this season of pain? Talk to My Father about this experience. What did He reveal to me?

3. Thinking especially of loved ones, have I ever stepped in to deliver anyone from his or her suffering? Explain. Was my intervention motivated by God? What resulted from my intervention?

4. Thinking of an experience I witnessed when someone endured intense suffering that resulted in good for them and for others, in the end, how did it bring glory to God?

Reflect on what I am saying, for the Lord will give you insight into all this.
(2 Timothy 2:7)

REPENTANCE

Lord God, my suffering seems unbearable at times and I've become bitter when I cry out to You for deliverance and You don't seem to respond. I've demonstrated a rebellious attitude when I've watched my loved ones suffer too, and felt as if You didn't care. I'm so sorry, righteous

Father, for the attitude of my heart. Take out this heart of stone and give me a heart of flesh. Renew a right spirit within me, God.

OTHER AREAS OF REPENTANCE

_____

_____

_____

Repent, then, and turn to God, so that your sins may be wiped out,
that times of refreshing may come from the Lord.
(Acts 3:19)

SUBMISSION

Lord Jesus, Lamb of God, You endured unimaginable suffering for the forgiveness of my sin so that I could be whole. Thank You, God, for Your great demonstration of love. Now Lord, I submit my life fully to You. Have Your way in me. Accomplish what You need to accomplish in me. Strengthen me by Your Spirit in my inner being to endure this season and use my life and my suffering to minister hope and healing to others. In Jesus' Name.

OTHER AREAS OF SUBMISSION

_____

_____

_____

Submit yourselves, then, to God.
(James 4:7)

FROM THE FATHER'S HEART

You are precious to Me, and My love for you will never change. Your willingness to lay down your life according to My perfect will delights Me. Your suffering will not be in vain, My beloved. Your pain will not endure forever, but My love for you surely will endure forever. Trust Me to take you through this season and receive My peace as we continue the journey. In the midst of your suffering, offer Me the sacrifice of praise, for the victory belongs to you!

PERSONAL WORD FROM MY FATHER

Speak, LORD, for your servant is listening.
(1 Samuel 3:9)

DAY 31

MEDITATION

Although the enemy has brought much destruction, tearing down that which is sacred in my life, God will restore what the enemy has destroyed. With God, all things are possible! When the manifestation of His restoration comes to pass, all will know that no man could have brought it to pass. Even those who have mocked and ridiculed the work of Your hand, will stand in awe of what You have done. The one and only true God will receive all glory, all honor and all praise.

May my meditation be pleasing to him, as I rejoice in the LORD.
(Psalm 104:34)

SCRIPTURE FOCUS

They realized this work had been done with the help of our God.
(Nehemiah 6:16, NLT)

What is my Father speaking to me through this Scripture?

_____

_____

_____

DEVOTION FOR THE DAY

It wasn't looking good for God's people. Decades after their exile in Babylon, Israel was allowed to return to their homeland, but the wall of Jerusalem had been torn down and its gates had been destroyed with fire. But God had a plan.

The prophet Nehemiah, cupbearer of the King of Persia, was grieved when he received word that those who survived the exile to Babylon were now in great trouble and disgrace. The fallen wall of Jerusalem, a bitter reminder of the consequences of Israel's sin, brought Nehemiah to his knees. He mourned, fasted and prayed for days. The wall needed to be rebuilt, reminding Israel of the blessing and restoration of their God's covenant people.

"O LORD, God of heaven," Nehemiah prayed, "the great and awesome God, who keeps his covenant of love with those who love him and obey his commands, let your ear be attentive and your eyes open to hear the prayer your servant is praying before you day and night for your servants, the people of Israel. I confess the sins we Israelites, including myself and my father's house, have committed against you. We have acted very wickedly toward you. We have not obeyed the commands, decrees and laws you gave your servant Moses.

"Remember the instruction you gave your servant Moses, saying, 'If you are unfaithful, I will scatter you among the nations, but if you return to me and obey my commands, then even if your exiled people are at the farthest horizon, I will gather them from there and bring them to the place I have chosen as a dwelling for my Name.'

"They are your servants and your people, whom you redeemed by your great strength and your mighty hand. O Lord, let your ear be attentive to the prayer of this your servant and to the prayer of your servants who delight in revering your name. Give your servant success today by granting him favor in the presence of this man" (Nehemiah 1:5-11).

God heard Nehemiah. Humbling himself before God, he had asked for help, then made himself available to be sent by God as the answer.

Covered with God's grace and fueled with purpose, Nehemiah received favor with the king, who released him to help the Jews, even sending letters to pave the way for the work needed when he arrived.

But opposition awaited Nehemiah as he moved forward with the huge undertaking to rebuild the wall. Troublemakers showed up, resolving to squelch God's plan. Displeased that Nehemiah had come to help the people of Israel, they tried to discourage Israel. "What does this bunch of poor, feeble Jews think they're doing?" they taunted. "Do they think they can build the wall in a single day by just offering a few sacrifices? Do they actually think they can make something of stones from a rubbish heap-and charred ones at that?"

Another added, "That stone wall would collapse if even a fox walked along the top of it."

But Nehemiah, knowing God's faithfulness, prayed, trusting God, reminding Him of how these enemies were mocking them and their God. Although the mumbling mockers continued throughout the reconstruction project, Nehemiah's work continued.

In just 52 days, less than two months, the wall was finished! And when Israel's enemies and surrounding nations heard about the wall, they were frightened and humiliated. *They realized this work had been done with the help of the God of Israel.*

When we humble ourselves and bring our petitions to God as Nehemiah did, He sometimes sends us as an answer to our own prayer.

For years, I sensed growing concern about increasing media reports of evil in the world. An overabundance of the works of darkness penetrated the nightly news, yet reports of the wondrous works of God were strangely absent.

I pounded the gates of heaven, crying out to God for change. "The devil has shown the world his best, but God, it's time for You to show off!" I prayed, pleading with Him to open avenues for His work to be spread across the nations.

God heard that prayer. And sent me as part of the answer.

A short time later, I began collecting and publishing God's miracle testimonies in the earth today. Surrendering to God's call to share His miracles with the world, I submitted myself to Him, willing to do whatever He asked of me.

But like Nehemiah, much opposition and challenge awaited me. As I started my previous book *Extraordinary Miracles in the Lives of Ordinary People*, I entered the most difficult season of my life. The full story is shared in my most recent book *From the Wilderness to the Miraculous* (Destiny Image Publishers).

Though I didn't know from day to day if I would live or die, and much discouragement came to bring the project to a halt, the work continued and God enabled me to complete the project with great success.

Those who had witnessed my journey of suffering through this long-term wilderness season knew what I myself knew better than anyone: *God did it*. This work could *only* have been completed with the help of our great God. To God be the glory!

When God sends you as an answer to your petitions, make yourself available. Though enemies may lie in wait to mock and bring your work to a halt, God will fuel you with strength and provide everything you need to get the job done. And like Nehemiah's work and my work, in the end, friend and foe will realize *this work has been done with the help of the God of Israel.*

FOR REFLECTION

1. What area of my life has been torn down and is in need of rebuilding? Consider family, friends, relationships, career, and emotional, physical and spiritual issues. Identify and document what has taken place and what is needed for rebuilding.

2. Regardless of the cause for the past destruction, have I shared my heart with my Father about what has been destroyed and have I forgiven those involved? Am I willing to be used by God for restoration?

3. As I set some time aside to process the emotions related to the above area, can I repent for the part I played in the destruction? Can I stand in the gap and ask God's forgiveness for others involved, including past generations? Repent before the Lord, ask Him to restore that which has been broken, and make myself available for the heavenly rebuilding project.

4. Do I believe God can restore what has been destroyed in the past? Am I willing to move forward in spite of mockers and those who doubt and ridicule me? Make God's restoration a matter of daily prayer, and ask God for wisdom regularly. He hears my prayer and is already at work on my behalf. Expect to see Him at work!

Reflect on what I am saying, for the Lord will give you insight into all this.
(2 Timothy 2:7)

REPENTANCE

God of all power and might, though I've been surrounded by destruction, I've failed to bring my concerns to You. Instead of asking You to bring restoration to that which has been left in ruins, I've complained. Instead of making myself available to You as a vessel to bring restoration, I've stood far off, assuming all had been lost. Dear God, forgive my sin! Forgive the error of my ways! I lay prostrate before You in repentance. I'm sorry, Father.

OTHER AREAS OF REPENTANCE

_____

_____

Repent, then, and turn to God, so that your sins may be wiped out,
that times of refreshing may come from the Lord.
(Acts 3:19)

SUBMISSION

O Lord, Most High God, I grieve at what the enemy has torn down in my life. Yet in spite of the loss, I believe that all things are possible with You. Lord, I kneel at Your throne, and ask You to rebuild and restore that which has been stolen. I make myself available to be used of You during the process of rebuilding. Send me as part of Your answer. Use me, Father, my life belongs to You. In Jesus' Name.

OTHER AREAS OF SUBMISSION

_____

_____

Submit yourselves, then, to God.
(James 4:7)

FROM THE FATHER'S HEART

I am the God of restoration and nothing is impossible for Me. I have waited for you to release that which appears to lie in ruins. Bring everything to Me, my trusted servant, even the broken pieces and the ashes. I will restore all things, turning your brokenness and ashes into a beautiful masterpiece that radiates My glory. As you build the foundation of your life on Me, nothing can shake you as you will be standing firm on the Solid Rock.

PERSONAL WORD FROM MY FATHER

_____

_____

_____

Speak, LORD, for your servant is listening.
(1 Samuel 3:9)

DAY 32

MEDITATION

When I submit to and commit to God's plan, I will face opportunities to become distracted. As I move forward in my Father's work, some may mock me, lie to me, lie about me, deceive me or manipulate me. I refuse to engage in skirmishes with the enemy. With my Father's help, I remain focused on His purpose, and with great joy I will complete the tasks He has given me. All will see that He is the God who makes the impossible possible.

May my meditation be pleasing to him, as I rejoice in the LORD.
(Psalm 104:34)

SCRIPTURE FOCUS

So I replied by sending this message to them: "I am engaged in a great work,
so I can't come. Why should I stop working to come and meet with you?"
Four times they sent the same message and each time I gave the same reply.
(Nehemiah 6:3-4, NLT)

What is my Father speaking to me through this Scripture?

_____

_____

_____

DEVOTION FOR THE DAY

Time is short. Jesus is coming soon. We can't afford to waste time engaging in skirmishes with the enemy.

In Day 31, we focused on the rebuilding of the wall of Jerusalem, the amazing reconstruction project that was completed in only 52 days. That project, however, could have been delayed, if not forever put on hold, had Nehemiah taken the devil's bait.

The project was near the end. The wall was complete and no gaps remained, but it still needed a few finishing touches. Only the doors had to be set up in the gates.

Nehemiah and those working with him had already endured the taunting of troublemakers Tobiah, Sanballat and Geshem the Arab, who tried to discourage them throughout the project. But the wall workers didn't take the bait. Plan A of the enemies hadn't worked, therefore the reconstruction project had moved forward.

Now, time was short and the project was close to completion. Desperate, Nehemiah's enemies went to Plan B. They sent Nehemiah a message: "Come, let us meet together in one of the villages on the plain of Ono" (Nehemiah 6:2).

But Nehemiah knew they were scheming to harm him; so he sent messengers to them with a reply: "I am carrying on a great project and cannot go down. Why should the work stop while I leave it and go down to you?" They didn't take no for an answer though. Four times they sent him the same message, and each time he gave them the same answer

(Nehemiah 6:3-4). Nehemiah had been invited into a skirmish with his enemy, but he didn't take the bait.

Plan B didn't work so now his enemy had to go to Plan C. A fifth message read, "It is reported among the nations—and Geshem says it is true—that you and the Jews are plotting to revolt, and therefore you are building the wall. Moreover, according to these reports you are about to become their king and have even appointed prophets to make this proclamation about you in Jerusalem: 'There is a king in Judah!' Now this report will get back to the king; so come, let us confer together" (vv. 6-7).

Nehemiah, once again refusing to take the bait, sent his reply: "Nothing like what you are saying is happening; you are just making it up out of your head" (v. 8). Instead of taking the bait, Nehemiah asked God to strengthen their hands to complete the work.

Plan C failed, so the enemy moved on to Plan D. Pulling an outside party into the plan, they hired a man to request a meeting with Nehemiah in the house of God, inside the temple, saying that men were coming to kill him (v. 10). But Nehemiah, again, refused to take the bait, going only to God, asking Him to deal with his enemies.

Having refused the enemy's bait to squelch God's work, the wall was completed right on time, in an amazing 52 days.

When we put our hand to the plow and begin the assignments with which God entrusts us, opposition will come to distract us. Like Nehemiah, the enemy will send people or circumstances our way to pull us into skirmishes, trying to take our focus off of our work. If we respond and give our attention to these distractions, we can get entangled in dealings with evil that can burn valuable time. As we stay the course, God will deal with our enemies.

As He enabled Nehemiah to rebuild the wall in 52 days, God is doing a quick work in His people today. Time is short. Jesus is coming soon. When the enemy presents you with Plan A, B, C, or D, don't take the bait! You have much work to do.

FOR REFLECTION

1. Reflecting on the building project identified in the Day 31 devotion, as I engage in God's rebuilding project, the enemy may attempt to distract me by luring me into senseless skirmishes. What possible distractions are ahead that could become stumbling blocks? Identify them.

2. In relation to the issues addressed in question #1, how can I prepare myself ahead of time to defuse these distractions if and when they present themselves?

3. Looking back, think of a time I became distracted while in the midst of fulfilling an assignment God had given me. Explain.

4. What was the outcome of my distraction? How much time, if any, was wasted? How can I avoid taking the devil's bait when he sets his schemes in motion to take my focus off of God and the project with which He has entrusted me?

Reflect on what I am saying, for the Lord will give you insight into all this.
(2 Timothy 2:7)

REPENTANCE

My Lord and my God, I fall on my knees with a heavy heart. At times I have willingly accepted the tasks You have given me, started strong, then finished weak, if at all. Forgive me for my unfaithfulness. Forgive me for taking Satan's bait, becoming snared in his schemes to distract me from

Your purpose. I'm sorry for sinning against You, dear Lord. Cleanse me and wash away my sin so I might start anew.

OTHER AREAS OF REPENTANCE

_____

_____

_____

Repent, then, and turn to God, so that your sins may be wiped out,
that times of refreshing may come from the Lord.
(Acts 3:19)

SUBMISSION

O, Father, I'm grateful that You are the God of second chances. Thank You for not giving up on me in spite of my past failures. As You continue reconstruction work in my life, I ask that You would align my heart with Your heart. Grant me wisdom, Lord of Hosts, and discernment to recognize distractions that strive to woo me away from Your plans and purposes. Enable me by Your Spirit to remain steadfast, focused on what You've asked of me, and unmoved by man's misguided words or actions. In Jesus' Name.

OTHER AREAS OF SUBMISSION

_____

_____

_____

Submit yourselves, then, to God.
(James 4:7)

FROM THE FATHER'S HEART

I grant abundant wisdom and discernment to you, Child, so walk therefore in it. Though opposition will come to drive you away from My work, I will keep your spiritual eyes open wide to recognize it. I will show you wolves clothed as sheep and will reveal schemes of the enemy, which come in many forms. Your eyes will be kept wide open as you keep your heart open wide to Me. As you walk with Me, nothing can delay or destroy what I am building.

PERSONAL WORD FROM MY FATHER

_____

_____

_____

Speak, LORD, for your servant is listening.
(1 Samuel 3:9)

DAY 33

MEDITATION

Regardless of where I am today, the great I AM, the God and Father of the Lord Jesus, desires fellowship with me. Whether I have sinned or have been deceived by the devil, my heavenly Father is waiting for my return. If I have drifted away, I can drift back into His arms today. Jesus, the spotless Lamb of God, made the way for my relationship to be restored with my loving Father.

May my meditation be pleasing to him, as I rejoice in the LORD.
(Psalm 104:34)

SCRIPTURE FOCUS

We must pay more careful attention, therefore,
to what we have heard, so that we do not drift away.
(Hebrews 2:1)

What is my Father speaking to me through this Scripture?

DEVOTION FOR THE DAY

It had been over 12 years since I had promised God that I would never drink alcohol again.

At the climax of my wilderness season, pain wracked my body around the clock. Physically and emotionally weak, I was troubled daily by the uncertainty of my future and the future of my loved ones. Determined to persevere in spite of my circumstances, I professed God's promises regularly and daily took communion.

Using grape juice to remember the blood Jesus shed for the forgiveness of my sins, and bread to remember His broken body that provided for my healing, I thanked God for the price He had paid for me. Daily I quieted myself before the Lord and meditated on Jesus, His death and resurrection.

In the midst of communion one day, a whisper arose in my heart. "I want you to use wine to celebrate communion."

But Lord! I prayerfully retaliated in thought, *I promised a long time ago that I would never drink alcohol!*

"That was a commitment you made, not something I asked of you," I sensed Him respond. "I came to bring liberty and freedom, not bondage."

I wrestled with the suggestion for the next 24 hours. It was true, I thought, that God had never asked me to make the commitment I had made. And it was true that He came to bring liberty, to set us free from bondage. Though I didn't feel peace about it, I decided to do what I believed God was directing me to do.

I had been duped! The devil, referred to as the deceiver (Revelation 20:10), had outwitted me in a time of weakness. That little teaspoon of wine in the communion cup led to many months of inner turmoil, guilt, and condemnation. Caught in the enemy's deceptive trap, I was tossed to and fro one day and sent drifting the next.

While drifting, God, through His amazing grace, rescued me by throwing me His life preserver, the Holy Spirit, who guides into all truth. The devil was right in saying that God had come to bring liberty and freedom, not bondage, but as he did with Jesus in the wilderness, he had twisted the truth. We are free indeed, as where the Spirit of the Lord is, there is **freedom** (2 Corinthians 3:17). But in that freedom, we can choose not only what is permissible, but what is beneficial (1 Corinthians 10:23). We are free to say "I can" and we're free to say, "I can, but I choose not to."

The devil has radar for any avenue through which he can gain access to our lives, most often coming at times of weakness. Satan, approaching Jesus after He had fasted for 40 days and nights, offered Him bread at a weak moment, twisting scripture as he enticed him into sin. He didn't hesitate to try his schemes on the Son of God and he will not hesitate trying his schemes on you, even if he has to come into a holy time in God's presence when you're celebrating communion!

My dear friend Delsie, who opened her home for me to write this book, reminisced one morning about her family's early fishing adventures. Enjoying the peaceful atmosphere, she said, they basked in the sun, enveloped by God's awesome creation. Drinking in their surroundings while waiting for an unsuspecting fish to nibble on their bait, they didn't always pay close attention to where their boat was going. That is, until they realized they were about to run aground!

Delsie's family had drifted. Floating away without paying attention to how far they had drifted, they nearly collided with disaster.

We too, can drift away if we get distracted and don't pay close attention to where we're going! When we drift away from God, especially in a weak moment, we're vulnerable to drifting right into the devil's traps. God doesn't want us to be duped by the devil. Second Corinthians 2:11 says, "We don't want to unwittingly give Satan an opening for yet more mischief—we're not oblivious to his sly ways!" (MSG).

In the first century, the anchor was used as an image of stability and safety.* If we anchor ourselves in Jesus, He will bring stability and strength to our lives. And if you get off course and happen to drift, God

---

* *NLT Study Bible,* note on Hebrews 6:19, p. 2093

will respond to your SOS call, ready and willing to throw you His personalized life jacket for rescue.

Drop anchor and invite Jesus into your boat. In Him, you'll never drift away!

FOR REFLECTION

1. Have I ever been duped by the devil? Explain the circumstances that led to this experience. Pay particular attention to the presence or lack of presence of peace during that time.

2. Have I ever experienced a season where I drifted away from God? Did it happen suddenly or was it so gradual that I wasn't consciously aware of it? Explain.

3. How did I eventually recognize and acknowledge that I had drifted from God? Am I drifting now? Is shame from unconfessed sin keeping me from approaching God?

4. Am I anchored in Jesus? Am I planted in Christian fellowship where I can grow and find accountability? If not, ask God to lead me by His Spirit where I belong. If I'm not certain, visit various functions and churches. God will make His plan clear as I move forward.

Reflect on what I am saying, for the Lord will give you insight into all this.
(2 Timothy 2:7)

REPENTANCE

I confess my sin to You, Lord God. I have no excuses. I cannot justify my errors. I have drifted away from You, Father. I admit it. I've been duped by the devil and have fallen away from You. I'm sorry, my Lord and Savior. I want to return to You now. I've backslidden, but now I want to slide back into Your arms. Rescue me again, Father, for my sin has been great. I draw near to You now, Father. Draw near to me. I need You more than ever.

OTHER AREAS OF REPENTANCE

_____

_____

_____

Repent, then, and turn to God, so that your sins may be wiped out,
that times of refreshing may come from the Lord.
(Acts 3:19)

SUBMISSION

Lord Jesus, though I have been ashamed of my poor behavior, You love me in spite of my behavior. I'm amazed that You love me 100%, even when I have failed. Your love is unchanging and I'm so grateful that You receive me when I don't deserve it. Though I've failed in so many ways, I ask that You would use my life to bring You glory. Though I've fallen into the enemy's traps, please use me to help others avoid the snares I've encountered. In Jesus' Name.

OTHER AREAS OF SUBMISSION

_____

_____

_____

Submit yourselves, then, to God.
(James 4:7)

FROM THE FATHER'S HEART

I shall use you, My Beloved. What you consider failings are no surprise to Me. I saw your entire life before it began. I know You better than you know yourself. What you may consider failures are opportunities for My glory to shine before man. What you may consider mistakes are opportunities for My grace and mercy to be displayed. Let me lift your shame, for the price has been paid. I love you, 100%. I always have and always will. That is who I AM.

PERSONAL WORD FROM MY FATHER

_____

_____

_____

Speak, LORD, for your servant is listening.
(1 Samuel 3:9)

DAY 34

MEDITATION

The greatest treasures I will ever discover on the earth are the treasures discovered in the darkness. Though I cannot explain it, I know in my heart that the most precious jewels emerge from the most difficult seasons of my life, if my heart is turned toward my Father. I can embrace Jesus in the darkness, knowing that He will give me treasures to bring new life to others.

May my meditation be pleasing to him, as I rejoice in the LORD.
(Psalm 104:34)

SCRIPTURE FOCUS

I will give you the treasures of darkness, riches stored in secret places,
that you may know that I am the LORD,
the God of Israel, who summons you by name.
(Isaiah 45:3)

What is my Father speaking to me through this Scripture?

DEVOTION FOR THE DAY

It was gone. Seeing the empty prongs that once held the diamond from my engagement ring, my mouth dropped. How would I tell my husband that the diamond I had worn since the day he proposed, was gone forever. My stomach sickened.

Hoping to find my lost gemstone, I tried to retrace my steps, but knew it would be nearly impossible, as I had flitted in all directions throughout the day. Where would I begin? I had run several errands around town and grocery shopped, visited a friend and chauffeured the kids to various activities. My diamond could have bounced off the ground anywhere.

Almost as an afterthought, I prayed. "Lord, You know where my diamond is, so would You send Your angels to find it and bring it back to me?" The very thought seemed impossible and my request almost seemed silly to me. Though my faith was undoubtedly weak, I chose to hope, even if half-heartedly, as the diamond had great sentimental value.

Putting my concerns about my missing diamond aside, I went on with my day, spiffying up the house before I started dinner. While preparing a family recipe, I headed to the garage, as I needed an ingredient from the spare freezer.

Opening the door leading into the garage, I felt around in the dark for the light switch. Flicking on the light, I glanced down as I usually did, making sure not to miss the step. There, in plain view on the cold cement floor, sat my diamond, glittering in the dust as if to announce its presence.

That wasn't the last time I lost a precious gem.

Our daughter Emily used to love the outdoors, favoring a park at the top of a big hill near our home. One sunny day, we climbed the hill and ventured into the park. After pushing her on the swings, teeter tottering and playing in the sand box, Emily was more than ready for a nap. And a bath!

Back home, while tucking her in, I noticed that one of her earrings was gone. "Emily!" I said. "Your earring is gone! Where is it?"

"I dunno," she said, then curled up for her snooze without a care. I had a care though. I wanted to find that earring, a diamond cross.

We retraced our steps later, walking up the right side of the street and down the other side. But we found no earring. Hoofing it up the hill again, we returned to the park area where we had played earlier. Zigzagging across the grounds, I inspected every spot of grass and dirt I could find. We searched the sandbox. But no earring.

Disappointed, I dropped my head and closed my eyes. Sighing, I knew I had given it my best effort and accepted the fact that the earring was lost forever.

Opening my eyes, a glitter in the sand caught my eye. Shimmering in the midday sun, the little cross earring sparkled, almost blinding me. And the earring back sat next to it, as if placed there intentionally.

Reaching down, I grasped the cross in my hand, holding it close to my chest. "Thank You, Jesus," I said with a sigh of relief and gratitude. "Thank You!"

God has hidden treasures for you in the dark of the night seasons. He has stored up riches for you in the sweltering seasons of the wilderness. He wants you to find new treasures, and old treasures you thought were lost forever!

As the sun shone its light to reveal the previously hidden cross in the sand, the Son will shine His light in the darkness to reveal the hidden treasures He has stored up for you. You are God's precious gem and nothing will *ever* snatch you out of His hand.

DAY 34

FOR REFLECTION

1. As I review my wilderness season, what treasures have I discovered this far into the journey?

2. Have I ever lost something that was precious to me? Explain. Did I find it or did I have to confront feelings of loss? How do I view this loss now?

3. What do I consider my treasures on this earth? With an open heart, what is most important to me?

4. What am I searching for? As I identify the desires of my heart, share them with my Father and ask Him to give me the desires of my heart.

Reflect on what I am saying, for the Lord will give you insight into all this.
(2 Timothy 2:7)

REPENTANCE

Father, I bow before You, acknowledging that I know so little about Your ways. I've begged to be delivered from this season of wilderness, yet I realize that You are doing much more than I realize, bringing change in me that is necessary to fulfill Your plan. Change me, Father. I'm no longer desperate to be delivered from my suffering, I'm desperate to become what You want me to become. Mold me. Make me into that which will bring glory to You.

OTHER AREAS OF REPENTANCE

_____

_____

_____

Repent, then, and turn to God, so that your sins may be wiped out,
that times of refreshing may come from the Lord.
(Acts 3:19)

SUBMISSION

Here I am, Father. I am here for You. I turn away from my ways, knowing my ways are not the path that leads to Your abundant life. I turn to You. I give myself to You for Your use. I am here, offering myself as a living sacrifice. Make me holy and acceptable to You. In Jesus' Name.

OTHER AREAS OF SUBMISSION

_____

_____

_____

Submit yourselves, then, to God.
(James 4:7)

FROM THE FATHER'S HEART

You are My greatest treasure. You are the apple of My eye. Do you know how much I love you? Do you know how much I search for you every moment of every day? I long for you. I love you! I have hidden treasures for you. Seek Me with all of your heart and you will discover the jewels of My righteousness and the glory of My presence. Receive My love!

DAY 34

PERSONAL WORD FROM MY FATHER

Speak, LORD, for your servant is listening.
(1 Samuel 3:9)

DAY 35

MEDITATION

If I am willing, I AM will accomplish wondrous works during my sojourn on earth. If I make myself available for whatever He desires, I make myself a tool in the Master's hand, something through which He can accomplish great and mighty works. Without Him, I can do nothing, but with Him nothing is impossible!

May my meditation be pleasing to him, as I rejoice in the LORD.
(Psalm 104:34)

SCRIPTURE FOCUS

"I am the Lord's servant," Mary answered. "May it be to me as you have said."
(Luke 1:38)

What is my Father speaking to me through this Scripture?

_____

_____

_____

DAY 35

DEVOTION FOR THE DAY

On January 9, 2010, on a flight from Orlando to Spokane, I pulled out my MP3 player, reclined my seat and closed my eyes. After spending the previous week attending a Morris Cerullo World Conference where I participated in meetings from morning until night for seven days, I was physically weary. Though filled to overflowing with rich teachings after a life-changing week, I looked forward to resting on the flight home.

But God had other plans. With great clarity, the Lord spoke to my heart with spiritual volume that exceeded the praise music playing in my ears. "You will write a book in man's month of love."

If I hadn't been in a public setting, I would have likely blurted out, "*One* month, Lord?! The *shortest* month of the year?"

February, man's month of love, as God so creatively put it, was only weeks away. Questions raced through my mind. *Where would I find the time? Where could I go with no distractions? How would it come to pass?*

With some idea of what Sarah might have felt after hearing she would give birth to Isaac in her old age, I laughed out loud! The thought of writing a book in one month seemed impossible; all of my previous books required up to two years to complete.

Crazy as it seemed, I knew I had heard the voice of the Good Shepherd. I had pledged long ago to obey whatever He asked of me, and this was no exception. God had always been faithful in the past to bring to pass everything He had asked of me, and I knew He would be faithful to bring it to pass once again.

"Be it unto me as You have said, Lord," I said, submitting in my heart. "Nothing is impossible with You." For the remainder of my flight, God downloaded specific instruction for a 40-Day Devotional to inspire and strengthen people in wilderness seasons.

The following week when I met my treasured friend, Delsie, for lunch, I shared my experience of receiving God's directive to write a book. Without hesitancy, she offered her home as a place for me to tuck myself away with no distractions.

Believing God was making provision for me to accomplish what He had asked, I accepted Delsie's generous invitation with thanks. With my husband's support, on February 1, I moved my belongings, Bibles and reference materials into Delsie's home.

My bedroom, in the lower level of Delsie's home, became the "Upper Room" where I waited on God, worshipped, and wrote. Some days I wrote throughout the day, and other days I wrote throughout the night. Some days I fought throbbing headaches, other days I enjoyed perfect health. Some days I was able to focus and other days I hit a writer's block. While I worked in the "Upper Room," Delsie selflessly prayed me through the month of February in her own "Upper Room" upstairs!

Because of previously scheduled engagements and book signings, I lost six entire days of writing. As the clock ticked away and anxiety came, God reminded me that this was *His* project; I was only the chosen vessel through which He would accomplish it.

At exactly 5:00 pm on February 28, the book you hold in your hands was complete! God, as always, brought to pass that which He had spoken.

The Virgin Mary was familiar with receiving a unique assignment from God. While pledged to be married to Joseph, the angel Gabriel visited her, bringing her news that God had chosen her to give birth to Jesus, the Son of God (Luke 1:26-38).

As a virgin, Mary knew it would be impossible for her to become pregnant. When she questioned Gabriel about that detail, He said that the Holy Spirit would come upon her and the power of the Most High would overshadow her. "For nothing is impossible with God" (Luke 1:37).

Mary accepted her assignment, submitting herself to God's plan in spite of how impossible that plan appeared. "I am the Lord's servant," she said. "May it be to me as you have said." And it came to pass, just as God said.

Has God given you an assignment that seems impossible? Though you may not understand all of the details and don't know how it could possibly unfold, He has chosen you as His vessel for this assignment. If you are a willing servant, He will bring it to pass just as He has said, because as Gabriel said, "*Nothing* is impossible with God."

FOR REFLECTION

1. What has God asked of me? What has He put on my heart to do? Paying particular attention to the things I may consider trivial or of little value, document what I believe God wants me to do.

2. Have I submitted to that which I believe God desires from me? What, if anything, stands in the way of my submission?

3. Do I understand why God is asking me to do this? If not, do I need to understand the details before I can say, "May it be to me as You have said"?

4. God is sovereign and chooses the vessels through which He will fulfill His plan. Am I prepared to be a willing vessel? Am I afraid to surrender all so He can do what He desires to do through me? I can share my fears with my Father. What did He speak to my heart?

Reflect on what I am saying, for the Lord will give you insight into all this.
(2 Timothy 2:7)

REPENTANCE

My Creator, how I've limited You through my stubborn refusal to believe that You could do something with my life. I'm sorry, Father, for trying to put You in a box and trying to limit what You could or could not do with me. You are the Potter, I am the clay. I've failed! Help me, dear God, to remember who You are and that I am Yours to form into that which will bring You honor.

OTHER AREAS OF REPENTANCE

Repent, then, and turn to God, so that your sins may be wiped out,
that times of refreshing may come from the Lord.
(Acts 3:19)

SUBMISSION

Oh Lord, nothing is impossible with You! I am so limited in every way. But when I am weak, You are strong. When I am a failure, You make me a victor! When I am weary, You bring me strength. Fill me to overflowing, Father God, with everything I need for life and godliness. I can live life to the fullest only through You! In Jesus' Name.

OTHER AREAS OF SUBMISSION

Submit yourselves, then, to God.
(James 4:7)

FROM THE FATHER'S HEART

You are My chosen one. I have raised you up for such a time as this. I have equipped you with everything you need to fulfill My divine plan. As you submit yourself to Me, I do the work. I will fill you, do you not know by now? You can do all things through Me! Nobody on the earth, not one, can fulfill that which I have called you to fulfill. Go for it, My child. For I am with you!

PERSONAL WORD FROM MY FATHER

Speak, LORD, for your servant is listening.
(1 Samuel 3:9)

DAY 36

MEDITATION

My Father is trustworthy. He is the author and finisher of my faith. He is the Alpha and the Omega. He is awesome in every way! I can put my trust in Him regardless of what trials visit my life. He is faithful. Always. He loves me. Always. If I know His love, I can trust Him and if I trust Him, I can rest in Him.

May my meditation be pleasing to him, as I rejoice in the LORD.
(Psalm 104:34)

SCRIPTURE FOCUS

You watched me as I was being formed in utter seclusion,
as I was woven together in the dark of the womb. You saw me
before I was born. Every day of my life was recorded in your book.
Every moment was laid out before a single day had passed.
(Psalm 139:15-16, NLT)

What is my Father speaking to me through this Scripture?

DEVOTION FOR THE DAY

"I was in an accident," Tom said, calling from a business trip in the Portland area. While driving to a last minute customer meeting in Longview, Washington, he had blown a tire on the I-5 freeway. After having the tire replaced at Les Schwab, he T-boned a Geo Metro that had pulled out in front of him as he turned out of the parking lot.

Much to my relief, Tom had not been hurt, nor had the driver of the other car suffered any injury. The young driver of the Geo Metro willingly admitted guilt and all was well—except that Tom's car needed major repair.

As a normal precaution after accidents, my husband's employer sent him to get checked out at the hospital. When they saw something out of the ordinary on his EKG, they directed him to see a doctor for further testing when he returned home to Spokane. Although he had brushed off any suggestion of injury, he had already been experiencing shortness of breath when climbing a hill behind our home where we normally walked.

The following week, because his car was in the shop, Tom had to cancel a business trip he had scheduled to visit customers in Billings, Montana. Though frustrating, God, the Master Planner, had orchestrated the change of plans. Since he was stuck at home that week, Tom followed up with his doctor as he had been advised. While Tom underwent a stress test, medical staff had to stop the test and administer nitroglycerin when he experienced difficulty breathing. He had failed the test.

"We're going to transfer him to the main surgery center for an angiogram," medical staff told me. A nurse called for me to sign papers, and then rattled off directions to the new surgical location. Timing was critical so they rushed Tom over to the surgical area immediately to further diagnose what might be causing the problems.

In the waiting room, I fanned through magazines and returned phone calls during what I had anticipated to be a simple procedure. Ending a call, I closed my cell phone when the surgeon came into the waiting area. "Party with Tom Marszalek?" he said, looking around.

I stood up, anxious for his debriefing. "It didn't look good in there, Mrs. Marszalek," he said. "One of the three main arteries to the heart was 98% blocked." To open the blockage, he had successfully inserted a stent and all had gone well.

"In a couple of days," the surgeon said before he disappeared through the waiting room door, "it would have been a massive heart attack."

In a couple of days, it would have been a massive heart attack, echoed through my mind.

Tom, who had planned to travel from Spokane to Billings that week, would have been covering sparse territory in the middle of nowhere. Having accompanied him on business trips in the past, I pictured the long stretches of road with its scenery of stark nothingness.

Had Tom not been in the accident the week before, his trip to Billings would have come to pass that week. Had he suffered a massive heart attack in the middle of nowhere, he would have been unable to get help. But God, who has the master plan and knows the beginning from the end, intervened and caused a change of plans.

The apparent disruption to Tom's agenda ended up being a temporary affliction that left as quickly as it had arrived. He breezed through surgery and was back on his feet, and back on the road, in no time.

Unexpected circumstances often side swipe us, frustrating our plans and agendas. God, the Author and Implementer of a master plan that He put in motion long before we were born, laid out every moment of our life before a single day passed!

Nothing that touches our life comes as a surprise to God. Regardless of what blowouts pop up along the road, God is well aware of it ahead of time and is in our tomorrows, orchestrating events before we arrive. Whatever you're facing today, it's no accident. The Master, has a master plan.

FOR REFLECTION

1. As I reflect on the more difficult challenges of my life, were any of these trials a blessing in disguise? Explain.

2. What was my attitude when faced with the challenges I mentioned?

3. What did I learn, if anything, from walking through the most difficult seasons of my life? Did I draw closer to God or did I drift further from Him? Why?

4. When I face trial, am I willing to trust God in spite of my circumstances? Why or why not?

Reflect on what I am saying, for the Lord will give you insight into all this.
(2 Timothy 2:7)

REPENTANCE

God, my God, how often I have thought that You had forsaken me! Yet in my darkest moments, You were there and You had a plan. Forgive me for stressing and wavering in my faith when trials confronted me. When all is well, it is so easy to trust You, but when trial comes, it hasn't been so easy for me. Help me develop my faith, Lord. I need You.

OTHER AREAS OF REPENTANCE

_____

_____

_____

Repent, then, and turn to God, so that your sins may be wiped out,
that times of refreshing may come from the Lord.
(Acts 3:19)

SUBMISSION

Lord Jesus, Giver of Life, I put my trust in You today. Regardless of what circumstances I will face today, I choose to give them to You, to trust You and to rest in You. Your love enables me to trust You. Thank You for loving me. Thank You for walking with me through the valley of the shadow of death. I can rest knowing You are with me, and will never leave me or forsake me. In Jesus' Name.

OTHER AREAS OF SUBMISSION

_____

_____

_____

Submit yourselves, then, to God.
(James 4:7)

FROM THE FATHER'S HEART

You are safe under the shadow of My wing. Nothing can take place in your life without it being filtered through Me. I am well aware of every detail. I have a plan for what you face today and I have a plan for what you will face tomorrow. My plan is a good plan. You can rest in Me because I love you! Everything is going be ok!

PERSONAL WORD FROM MY FATHER

_____

....

....

Speak, LORD, for your servant is listening.
(1 Samuel 3:9)

DAY 37

MEDITATION

My God, my God, You have not forsaken me! I rejoice today that my Lord and Savior paved the way for my emotional, physical and spiritual healing. I receive it by faith now. Today I am set free! Today I am healed. Today, my wounds are healed by the wounds Jesus endured for my sake. I receive it today!

May my meditation be pleasing to him, as I rejoice in the LORD.
(Psalm 104:34)

SCRIPTURE FOCUS

He heals the brokenhearted and binds up their wounds.
(Psalm 147:3)

What is my Father speaking to me through this Scripture?

_____

_____

_____

DEVOTION FOR THE DAY

"Wasn't he just born?" I asked Tom. I felt so proud watching James graduate from Basic Training at Fort Knox, soon to be headed for his tour of duty in Iraq. I was melancholy too, realizing how the years had flown by.

At the airport, we went in different directions, us headed to Spokane and James headed to his military station in Fairbanks, Alaska. We were delighted when the airlines upgraded James to first class, honoring and thanking him for his service to our country.

We huffed it to our gate lugging James' Army duffle bag, which was full of the belongings he asked us to store while he was overseas. Tom and I chatted while waiting for our return flight to depart, Tom's chest puffed out with pride, donning his new t-shirt that bore our son's unit insignia.

"Excuse me, sir," a woman said, tapping Tom on the shoulder. "I want to thank you for serving our country, sir." Her tearful gratitude touched my heart. Smiling through her watery eyes, she walked away, disappearing down the walkway before we had a chance to let her know that our son, not Tom, was serving in the military.

Tears brimmed in Tom's eyes in response to the woman's words. Seeing Tom's t-shirt and the Army duffle bag at his side, the stranger had assumed that he was military personnel. She came and left so fast that we weren't able to correct her mistake.

It wasn't, however, a mistake.

In February of 1973, Tom and an aircraft full of fellow comrades were en route to the United States after serving in the Vietnam War. The pilot announced that although they were initially scheduled to fly into Travis Air Force Base in California, they would instead land at San Francisco International. At the time, San Francisco was the epicenter of radical, dope smoking, anti-war, free love, tie-dye long hairs.

Dressed in their Class A uniforms that proudly displayed brass shining, ribbons and combat patches, the returning vets were excited to be heading back to the good ole USA after their tour in Vietnam. They weren't anticipating the reception they were about to encounter.

As the servicemen deplaned, hostile men and women dressed in headbands and sandals, wearing raggedy clothes, shook their fists while screaming obscenities. "War mongers! Baby killers!" they yelled while spitting in the soldiers' faces. One spit glob hit Tom in the temple and another smack dab on his left breast, covering the ribbons he had displayed so proudly only moments ago.

After hustling through the gauntlet of protestors, Tom headed to the restroom so he could change out of his uniform to be less conspicuous. However, the only "hip" clothes he was able to buy in the PX on Tan Son Nhut Air Base back in Saigon, were a purple long sleeve shirt, bellbottom jeans and sandals. Tom entered the men's room a soldier and exited a PX hippie.

"Tom," I said, realizing what God had done. "You *did* serve our country. Those words were meant for *you*." Overcome with emotion, Tom couldn't speak. God had used this unknowing woman to bring healing and bind up wounds inflicted 35 years earlier by those who made false accusations and didn't recognize the price that was paid for freedom.

Jesus understood what Tom and his comrades experienced as they deplaned in San Francisco. Jesus came to serve, willingly leaving His heavenly dwelling to come to the earth to save men from their sin. Yet those He came to save yelled, "Crucify Him!" Those for whom He died, beat Him, spit in His face, blindfolded Him, mocked and insulted Him, flogged Him, struck Him with their fists, struck Him on the head again and again, and finally killed Him (Matthew 26:67, 27:30, Mark 10:33-34, Luke 18:32). Yet His unfailing love enabled Him to say, "Forgive them, Father, for they know not what they do" (Luke 23:34).

Jesus paid a great price to heal the brokenhearted and bind up their wounds. Where the Spirit of the Lord is, there is freedom (2 Corinthians 3:17). Christ paid a great price for that freedom. Do as the stranger did with Tom. Tap Jesus on the shoulder and say, "Thank you, Jesus, for serving. Thank you, Jesus, for the price You paid for my freedom."

FOR REFLECTION

1. What price did Jesus pay for my freedom from sin, sickness, disease, shame, and sorrow? What penalty was paid for my peace?

2. Have I received God's gift in Jesus? When did I receive His gift? Explain the details. If I have not received Jesus and the gift of eternal life through the forgiveness of my sin, do I want to receive it now? I can repent of my sin right now and invite Him into my heart to dwell forever.

3. Do I have unhealed wounds from the past? Am I willing to allow Jesus to touch those wounds now? I can invite Him to heal my wounds and accept the path to healing that He has planned for me. I am free! I am healed!

4. Thank God for the gift of His Son! Thank You, Father, for the healing You have brought to my life through the blood of Your only begotten Son. Thank You for past healing, the healing You are doing today and the healing that will come in the future.

Reflect on what I am saying, for the Lord will give you insight into all this.
(2 Timothy 2:7)

REPENTANCE

Will You forgive me, Father, once again? How many times I have come to You for forgiveness, yet here I am again. I am in awe that Your mercy is new every morning. I have taken You for granted. I have taken the sacrifice Jesus made for me for granted. Oh God, what a price He paid for my freedom from the penalty of sin! I'm sorry God, I'm so sorry for grieving Your heart as I have. Cleanse me, Father. Wash my sin away so I might stand in the righteousness You provided at Calvary.

OTHER AREAS OF REPENTANCE

Repent, then, and turn to God, so that your sins may be wiped out,
that times of refreshing may come from the Lord.
(Acts 3:19)

SUBMISSION

Fill my heart with understanding of the price Your Son paid for my freedom. Enable me to live a life demonstrating that understanding and drawing others to the cross. You have saved me from the penalty of my sinfulness. You have given me freedom and liberty. You have set me free and I am free indeed. Use me now, Lord God, to lead the lost to You, the only source of hope. In Jesus' Name.

OTHER AREAS OF SUBMISSION

Submit yourselves, then, to God.
(James 4:7)

FROM THE FATHER'S HEART

I so loved you that I sent My Son to save you. How I long for you to know the fullness of My love. As you walk with Me, and write My Word on the tablet of your heart to lead and guide you, the understanding you desire will increase. The price My Son paid on your behalf was a great price indeed, but it was paid willingly with My love for I AM love.

PERSONAL WORD FROM MY FATHER

Speak, LORD, for your servant is listening.
(1 Samuel 3:9)

DAY 38

MEDITATION

It is as important for me to obey God when He directs me to stand still as it is to obey when He directs me to take action. I hear the voice of my Good Shepherd. I know His voice and I will follow Him. I can and will be still and know He is God.

May my meditation be pleasing to him, as I rejoice in the LORD.
(Psalm 104:34)

SCRIPTURE FOCUS

Enter his gates with thanksgiving; go into his courts with praise.
Give thanks to him and praise his name.
(Psalm 100:4, NLT)

What is my Father speaking to me through this Scripture?

_____

_____

_____

DEVOTION FOR THE DAY

Video games and computer games didn't exist when I was growing up. Instead of sitting in front of the television for hours on end, we played outside from morning until night, stopping only if we were called home for dinner. Instead of *Mario Kart,* we played Red Rover. Instead of *Halo,* we played kick ball. Instead of *Roller Coaster Tycoon,* we played softball and instead of *Need for Speed,* we ran real races.

I liked races especially, as I had long legs and could run fast. The command start was like music to my ears. Hearing, "On your mark," I'd get in my lane. With, "Get set," I'd get into position. "Go!" sent me running like a horse out of the gate, making a mad dash for the finish line. Although I won most of the races, I don't recall receiving a prize. Considering I was about a foot taller than my friends, I must admit it wasn't exactly fair anyway.

The three-command start for our childhood races provoked us to action. God seems to use a similar command start when He provokes us to action. Energizing us with His fuel and driving us with His purpose, He positions us in our lane, prepares us, and then sends us off with a bang! We do our part, and He does His part.

Sometimes, however, God throws us a curve ball and says, "On your mark. Get set. Stop!" Though that command can seem to trip us up when we're prepared to leave the starting gate, it creates an opportunity for God to show up and show off. Especially when we find ourselves in a jam.

King Jehoshaphat found himself in a sticky jam when the Moabite, Ammonite and Meunite army was headed his way to make war against Israel. (2 Chronicles 20:1-30.) Alarmed, he inquired of the Lord for direction and proclaimed a fast for all of Judah. After reminding God of His greatness and acknowledging their weakness and inability to face the vast army that was about to attack, he waited on the Lord.

Speaking through Jahaziel, God said they need not be afraid, as this battle did not belong to Israel. The battle belonged to the God of Israel.

Providing divine strategy, God revealed when, where and how to find their enemy. Providing a surprising side note, God said, "You will not have to fight this battle. Take up your positions; stand firm and see the deliverance the LORD will give you" (v. 17). Hearing the Word of the Lord, they bowed down in praise.

The next morning, Jehoshaphat implemented God's plan. While encouraging his men to put their faith in God, he appointed some to lead the army into battle with songs of praise to the Lord, acknowledging the splendor of his holiness.

"Give thanks to the LORD, for his love endures forever," they sang, marching toward the battlefield (vv. 20-21). As they praised the Lord, God set ambushes against some of their enemies, and defeated them. The remaining enemies rose up against each other until they were all destroyed (vv. 22-23). God's people, who had not lifted a finger against their enemy, found only dead bodies lying on the ground; no one had escaped! (V. 24.) It required three days for Jehoshaphat and his men to carry off the plunder! (V. 25.)

Israel's great victory was preceded by praises to God, and was followed by praise to God (vv. 26-28). Word spread like wildfire that the Lord, the God of Israel had fought against the enemies of Israel (v. 29).

If you find yourself in a jam when enemies seem to be closing in on every side, seek God for the battle plan, knowing that some battles belong to Him and Him alone. God may tell you, as He did Jehoshaphat: Get in position; stand firm, then see the deliverance the Lord will give you! Then sit back while you sing praises to the God of Israel. Without you lifting a finger, HE will destroy your enemies so you can run with perseverance the race marked out for you.

On your mark. Get set. Praise!

FOR REFLECTION

1. Am I in a jam? Explain.

2. Have I asked God for direction? Have I asked Him for wisdom? If so, what has He directed me to do? I can talk to my Father about my situation and ask Him for His plan and strategy. What has the Lord revealed to me?

3. Has God asked me now, or has He ever directed me to stand still when all walls seem to be closing in on me? Did I obey? What happened as a result of my obedience or disobedience?

4. What does, "This battle belongs to the Lord" mean to me? If my battle belongs to the Lord, am I willing to stand still?

Reflect on what I am saying, for the Lord will give you insight into all this.
(2 Timothy 2:7)

REPENTANCE

Father God, my wondrous God! You have opened my eyes to see where I've gone wrong. How often I have launched into action when Your desire was for me to stand still and how often I've stood still when I should have responded to Your call to action. I'm sorry, Lord, for taking matters into my own hands when You wanted to take matters into Your able hands. Only You know what is best, Lord. I want to go when You want me to go and stand still when You want me to be still. God Almighty, I have failed without You and cannot do this without Your help. Help me, O God!

OTHER AREAS OF REPENTANCE

_____

_____

_____

Repent, then, and turn to God, so that your sins may be wiped out,
that times of refreshing may come from the Lord.
(Acts 3:19)

SUBMISSION

Holy Lord, You know the best way. You know the only way to life abundant. I want Your plan. I want Your strategy. I surrender my strategies and plans to You, acknowledging that I do not know the best way in which to act. When You tell me to "Go" I will go and when You tell me to "stand still" I will stand still. My battles belong to You, Most High God. Give me Your battle plans, Lord, and I will follow. In Jesus' Name.

OTHER AREAS OF SUBMISSION

_____

_____

_____

Submit yourselves, then, to God.
(James 4:7)

FROM THE FATHER'S HEART

I protect you because I love you. My love for you is outrageous. My love is radical! I always have your best interest in mind. At times I will ask you to move and I delight when you move. But at times I will ask you to step aside and do nothing but trust Me. When I ask you to stand still, obey My voice. As you obey Me, you will see the wondrous works of My hand. Do not fear the enemies before you. When your enemies arise, I will act on your behalf, and your enemies will be scattered.

PERSONAL WORD FROM MY FATHER

Speak, LORD, for your servant is listening.
(1 Samuel 3:9)

DAY 39

MEDITATION

God will take everything the enemy meant for evil and use it for my good, the good of others, and for His glory. I need not be ashamed of my seasons of suffering but can rejoice in God's faithfulness throughout my trials. As I share my testimony of the comfort God gave me, it brings comfort to others. The God of all comfort will use me to bring comfort to others, if I am willing.

May my meditation be pleasing to him, as I rejoice in the LORD.
(Psalm 104:34)

SCRIPTURE FOCUS

Praise be to the God and Father of our Lord Jesus Christ, the Father
of compassion and the God of all comfort, who comforts us in all our troubles,
so that we can comfort those in any trouble with the comfort we ourselves
have received from God. For just as the sufferings of Christ flow over
into our lives, so also through Christ our comfort overflows.
(2 Corinthians 1:3-5)

What is my Father speaking to me through this Scripture?

_____

_____

_____

DEVOTION FOR THE DAY

She seemed distraught within, though outward appearances portrayed a stunning woman of confident stature. It wasn't necessary for her to tell me why she had come to the altar for prayer, as her need seemed obvious to me. Laying my hand on her shoulder, I began to pray silently. Sensing intense inner pain, it seemed as if God had enabled me to step into her shoes and experience her agony, hopelessness and pain. Moved with compassion, I wept. And she wept.

In a holy moment, God showed me a large drawing board covered with scribbling. An eraser then appeared, blotting out every scribble from top to bottom, wiping the slate clean. Satan had written lies on this woman's heart, the Lord revealed. When she came into agreement with those lies, it provided an avenue for depression to take root. But God was erasing the enemy's lies and was writing His message of love on her heart. Depression had to flee!

Wrapping her in my arms, I continued to pray and she continued to cry. I understood what she was feeling, as I had been in her shoes in days gone by. As if Jesus was embracing her through my arms, I sensed His compassion flow. I held God's daughter for a long time as He performed a miracle in her heart.

As we stood in His presence that day, God set that woman free, loosing her from the bonds of depression. In an instant, God accomplished what years of counseling could have never done. With great joy, I watched her leave a free woman.

I can spot depression from a distance, as its repulsive presence is familiar to me. The black looming cloud had visited my life not a few times. Though I insisted that this unwelcome guest leave after barging into my life uninvited, I didn't regret that it had visited. If not for my battle with depression, I would have missed the valuable treasures it left behind.

Although I had experienced significant long-term physical suffering over a long-term wilderness season, depression, to me, was considerably worse. "If I had to choose," I once told a pastor, "between enduring those five years of physical suffering all over again, or experiencing a two week episode of depression, I'd choose the five years of physical suffering." Hands down, there would be *no* competition.

The pastor didn't seem to understand. Like many types of suffering, unless one has experienced depression themself, it's not easy to understand, or to have compassion for those in the midst of it.

Depression, like many types of suffering is hellacious. Like many types of suffering, its debilitating physical, emotional and spiritual symptoms are many. It hurts. And even in the 21st century, depression, like many types of suffering, continues to be misunderstood.

Others may not understand the troubles you face right now, but the God of all comfort, the Father of Compassion understands your pain.

My compassionate Father comforted me in my suffering whenever depression dropped in unannounced. Now, moved with compassion, I can comfort others who receive a visit from the same unwelcome visitor with the comfort I received from Him. Moved with compassion, God will move heaven and earth to bring comfort when any kind of suffering knocks on our door, then barges in.

As you endure seasons of suffering, receive comfort from the God of all comfort. Let the Father of Compassion take you to the drawing board to write a new message on your heart. As you receive His comfort, He will enable you to comfort others who are suffering with the comfort you received from Him. You, like Jesus, and me, will be moved with compassion to bring healing and hope to set the captives free.

FOR REFLECTION

1. What area of major suffering have I endured and found victory through Christ? Explain.

2. Am I willing to openly share my journey through suffering addressed in question #1? If I have encountered others facing similar circumstances, have I taken the opportunity to share my testimony?

3. If I have hesitated to share my testimony, am I ashamed to reveal my experience or do I fear others will view me as weak? What needs to happen in order for me to be free to share my story?

4. What is the primary message written on the chalkboard of my heart? Does the message reveal the heart of God or does it reveal lies of the enemy? If issues of shame or rejection are written on my chalkboard, ask God to erase them by His Spirit and to replace them with His message of love.

Reflect on what I am saying, for the Lord will give you insight into all this.
(2 Timothy 2:7)

REPENTANCE

God, I have been selfish in keeping my testimony hidden. You delivered me, yet I've kept silent about You, my Deliverer! I've feared that revealing the areas with which I've struggled might make me appear weak or unstable to others. Pride has gripped me, Father, and though I didn't see it before, I see it clearly now. As I humble myself before You, please wipe away my sin. Forgive me of my sin, O Lord.

OTHER AREAS OF REPENTANCE

_____

_____

_____

Repent, then, and turn to God, so that your sins may be wiped out,
that times of refreshing may come from the Lord.
(Acts 3:19)

SUBMISSION

Holy Father, thank You for walking with me through the wilderness seasons. As I ponder Your greatness, I stand in awe of You, wondrous God. You've had compassion on me and have comforted me, even when I didn't know You were there and didn't deserve Your attention. I am willing, Lord, to share the testimony of Your goodness to anyone You bring across my path. As You open the door for me to share, I am ready in season and out. Use me to comfort others with the comfort You have given me. In Jesus' Name.

OTHER AREAS OF SUBMISSION

_____

_____

_____

Submit yourselves, then, to God.
(James 4:7)

FROM THE FATHER'S HEART

I am always here to comfort you. My love for you and for others motivates compassion and comfort. All of heaven stands at attention when My Name is being honored. You bring honor to My Name as You tell others what I have done for you. Let me fill you with My love. Let Me fill you with My compassion. Let Me fill you with My comfort. Now go, pour out what I have poured into you, into others. Then come, My child, and let me fill you more.

PERSONAL WORD FROM MY FATHER

Speak, LORD, for your servant is listening.
(1 Samuel 3:9)

DAY 40

MEDITATION

I do not know the day or the hour of Jesus' return, nor do I know the day or the hour my life on earth will come to a close. I will live every day as if it is my last and will make every moment matter.

May my meditation be pleasing to him, as I rejoice in the LORD.
(Psalm 104:34)

SCRIPTURE FOCUS

"Yes, I am coming soon." Amen. Come, Lord Jesus.
(Revelation 22:20)

What is my Father speaking to me through this Scripture?

DEVOTION FOR THE DAY

"He's coming soon!" I'd tell the kids while marking off calendar days leading up to Uncle Jim's visits. Ever since I relocated to Seattle, then Spokane, Jim had visited from Minneapolis at least once every year, making special effort to attend landmark events. Having Uncle Jim in our home was always a special treat for the kids as they loved him dearly—and he often treated them to Dairy Queen!

Being lonesome for family back home, I treasured Jim's visits as well. Jim and I, only one year apart, had been close for many years. Mom, Dad and I had established our traditional Sunday evening phone calls when I moved west, and when they passed away, Jim and I continued that tradition and still do to this day. I tease Jim occasionally, claiming that I'm still in counseling to recover from the painful discovery that he had dismantled my brand new red tricycle and never put it back together again!

Since my relocation, I have enjoyed many opportunities to visit family in Minneapolis, creating priceless memories of which Jim was often a part. On one trip home, Jim and I watched Jack Van Impe's television program together. I had never seen nor heard Jack Van Impe, and was amazed at his ability to quote scripture. I wondered if He had memorized the entire Bible! I listened carefully as Jack shared current events, then paralleled them with end time Biblical prophecy.

God opened my spiritual eyes and ears. "Jesus is coming soon!" Jack said throughout the 30-minute program. As he proved his words with scripture, my heart sank when a realization hit me. *Jesus is coming soon, and I'm not ready for His return!*

I flew back to Spokane a changed person. *Jesus is coming soon. Very soon.* Surrendering my life to Him, a new fervor saturated my soul. Wanting to be a tool in His hands, I was willing to do anything and everything the Lord asked to prepare myself, and others, for His impending return.

I had been expecting Joseph, our youngest son, during that life changing trip to Minneapolis, and suspected that because Christ would return first, Joe wouldn't be born on earth. My enquiring mind wondered how God was going to work that out. Jesus didn't return when I thought, however. Joe just turned 17!

"Tell my people that I'm coming soon!" the Lord whispered as I sought Him near the completion of this book. *Jesus is coming soon!* If you are not ready for Him, make yourself ready now, as He will come when you least expect it.

Before Christ returns, strange signs will appear in the sun, the moon and stars, and here on earth the nations will be in turmoil, perplexed by the roaring seas and strange tides. People will be terrified at what they see coming upon the earth, for the powers in the heavens will be shaken. Then *everyone* will see Jesus coming on a cloud with power and great glory (Luke 21:25-27). When all these things begin to happen, fear not! Stand and look up, for your salvation is near!" (Luke 21:28.)

Jesus is coming soon! Be alert! "Remain in fellowship with Christ so that when he returns, you will be full of courage and not shrink back from him in shame" (1 John 2:28, NLT).

If you don't know Jesus, He stands at the door of your heart and knocks. If you invite Him in, He will come in to dwell, cleanse you of sin and prepare you for a secure eternity with Him. If you've fallen away, your Father stands with open arms to welcome you back. "Come," He says, "I forgive you. I love you!"

As the Bible closes the book of Revelation, I close this book. Hear the Word of the Lord: "'Yes, I am coming soon.' Amen. Come, Lord Jesus" (Revelation 22:20).

FOR REFLECTION

1. If I died today, am I confident that I would spend eternity with my Father in heaven? Why or why not? Explain.

2. Do I fear the return of Jesus or do I anticipate it with joy and peace? Why or why not? Explain.

3. If Jesus returned today, am I ready for His return? Why or why not? What do I need to do to prepare myself for His return?

4. If I had only one week left on earth, would I live differently than I do now? Do I need to ask someone's forgiveness or forgive others? Have I done what I believe God has asked of me? If not, what has been left undone? List what comes to the surface as I ponder these issues and act on what God has revealed to me.

Reflect on what I am saying, for the Lord will give you insight into all this.
(2 Timothy 2:7)

REPENTANCE

Master, I often forget that life on earth is but a tiny slice of time and that eternity is forever. I'm sorry, Lord Jesus, for living my life so recklessly, making issues of things that don't matter and not making issues of things that do matter. I need to change, Lord. Help me to change and renew my mind so that I can make a difference in Your Kingdom. Help me prepare my heart and life for Jesus' return.

OTHER AREAS OF REPENTANCE

_____

_____

_____

Repent, then, and turn to God, so that your sins may be wiped out,
that times of refreshing may come from the Lord.
(Acts 3:19)

SUBMISSION

Father God, only You know the hour of Your Son's return. I receive Jesus today, and will receive Him every day anew, knowing that because of Him, I will spend eternity with You. I submit myself to You, Lord, and ask You to help me daily in fulfilling Your plan. Though I have many plans in my heart, I want Your plan to prevail. I don't want to leave anything You've asked of me undone. Change my heart, O God, and make me more like You. In Jesus' Name.

OTHER AREAS OF SUBMISSION

_____

_____

_____

Submit yourselves, then, to God.
(James 4:7)

FROM THE FATHER'S HEART

I've watched you, even while you were being formed in your mother's womb and I've watched you every moment of your life on earth. I loved you from the beginning and love you today. How I long to

be with you in eternity. How I long for you to share My heavenly glory. The One who made it possible for us to spend eternity together, My Beloved Son, is coming soon. I love you, My child. How I love you and long to say, "Well done, My good and faithful servant!" Then we will live together in My eternal glory forever and ever.

PERSONAL WORD FROM MY FATHER

_____

_____

_____

Speak, LORD, for your servant is listening.
(1 Samuel 3:9)

ABOUT THE AUTHOR

In addition to being an ordained minister, Therese Marszalek is a dynamic inspirational speaker and author. She has a master's of divinity degree from Shalom Bible College and Seminary and completed Rhema Bible School.

Founder of Therese Marszalek Ministries, Therese developed and taught discipleship and Christian writing classes where she finds great joy inspiring others to fulfill their God given destiny. Her message challenges people to walk closer with Christ, yet breathes healing and hope to the discouraged and weary. Her personal experience of searching for Christian truth and longing for a more intimate relationship with Christ birthed her speaking and writing ministry, as well as her zeal for discipleship in the body of Christ. Known for her unique transparency and spiritual depth, Therese draws her audience to a place of vulnerability where God can do His greatest work of transformation.

With hundreds of articles in print as a columnist and contributor to numerous books and television productions, Therese's writing and speaking ministry have reached across the globe to bring a message of hope in Christ. Her books include *From the Wilderness to the Miraculous* (Destiny Image), *Extraordinary Miracles in the Lives of Ordinary People* (Harrison House), *Miracles Still Happen* (Harrison House), and *Breaking Out* (Publish America).

Therese lives in Deer Park, Washington.

For more information or to contact Therese Marszalek:

Web site: www.theresemarszalek.com and
www.breakingoutministries.com

E-mail: therese.marszalek@gmail.com

Or write to:
Therese Marszalek
21616 No. Spotted Road
Deer Park, WA 99006

OTHER BOOKS BY THERESE MARSZALEK:

From the Wilderness to the Miraculous (Destiny Image)

Extraordinary Miracles in the Lives of Ordinary People
(Harrison House)

Miracles Still Happen (Harrison House)

Breaking Out (Publish America)